Long, White *&* Cloudy

Long, White & Cloudy

In search of a Kiwi spirituality

John Bluck

First published 1998
Copyright © 1998 John Bluck

The author asserts his moral rights in the work.

ISBN 1-877161-43-8

Published by Hazard Press
P.O. Box 2151, Christchurch, New Zealand
Production and design by Orca Publishing Services Ltd
Edited by Anna Rogers
Front cover photograph by Garth Des Forges and MOART
Author photograph by Garth Des Forges
Printed by Spectrum Print Ltd, Christchurch

Contents

Acknowledgements

My gratitude to the community at Christchurch Cathedral
for their encouragement on a shared journey, to Elizabeth,
for the title and much else, and to Nigel and Jessica,
whose images on film help me find words in print.

Foreword

I am a Christian but more and more I sense that Christianity too often finds itself at the margins of society, sharing its concerns with the few who want to listen. Belief, seemingly a statement about God, also serves to define those who are within the camp and those whose status is more problematic.

But it is those problematic ones who could be the salvation of the church. Their invitation is to come on over and understand us. Furthermore, these same people, as well as having needs, may also have insights. They may not dress it up in clear theological language but some of them have a sense of the place and purpose of God.

John Bluck puts himself in the middle of this rich and sometimes confusing Kiwi experience, describes its potential and shortfalls and then offers a spiritual dimension which could ground it within a reality and a sense of purpose we are all looking for.

I call it a spiritual dimension, for in a multi-ethnic and diverse New Zealand society Christianity is not the only spiritual tradition on the block. Christianity should no longer live by an assumption that it is nearer to truth than anyone else. Christianity's task is not to deny the reality of other people's sense of God but to listen, to learn and to clarify.

As always John Bluck writes clearly and with great perception. When I was a very young Bishop of Waiapu he was the first person I ordained to the priesthood. John has taught me a lot, especially about getting to the realities that lie within and beyond the things we tussle with. In other words, he gives me a sense of hope.

The Rt Revd Sir Paul Reeves
August 1998

Introduction

I can't think of a better time to write about spirituality in Aotearoa New Zealand. Allegiance to institutional religion is shaky, especially among young people, yet curiosity about the things of the spirit has never been stronger, especially among the young. That spiritual curiosity extends readily into issues of national identity, particularly for Pakeha people as they watch the renaissance of Maori culture and wonder why their own seems so elusive.

In the wider framework of Western culture, the time is right for an exploration of Kiwi spirituality. A decade ago, it may have seemed too parochial a topic, or simply premature. Today there is a worldwide hunger for understandings of the spirit that are well anchored and proudly owned; spiritualities that belong somewhere so that they can eventually be shared everywhere. For too long, we have laboured with spiritual theories imported and sold as being universally applicable, only to find that they were really designed for use in England, or India, or Southern California.

It's also a time of spiritual vacuum, in Western culture at least. The brave new worlds offered by science and technology, which promised to make the spirit redundant by the end of this century, have failed to arrive. Nuclear power and the ecological crisis warn us that it's dangerous to keep waiting. World councils, governments, trade unions, religions and experts of every kind have failed to make the common interests of our common humanity attractive enough for long enough to address the age-old issues of poverty and war. Some of us may be able to converse globally on the Internet, but 800 million people still can't afford to eat and a good number of them still live under threat of violence. The old absolutes and certainties from the time before Darwin and Einstein and Freud won't return.

In the midst of that turmoil, the longing for new forms of being and knowing wells up in the most surprising places, especially in those people once cynical about any spiritual dimension to life. The hunger for unity, wholeness and integration is encountered everywhere. And the dimensions of faith that point to the mystery of the divine life in and all around us prove increasingly attractive.

It's easy to show that Kiwi spirituality is a topical subject. It's much harder to know how to begin the search for some common ground that is open to all types and persuasions of spirituality. I fear this book may offend many people of orthodox religious faith, but they're not my primary audience. I'm trying to write for those spiritually curious New Zealanders who are uncommitted or uncertain about getting involved with any of the religious traditions, whether Christian or other living faiths.

The offence will come from the open-ended nature of what is said. A Kiwi spirituality, it seems, can include just about anything and anyone. Where are the safeguards? This book deliberately offers very few. After a lifetime of working inside several very traditional churches, my conviction is that many Christians, at least, are trapped in a defensive and protective mentality about their faith that leaves them overstating their claims, overreacting to criticism, constantly offering more than is asked for and promising more certainty than can be believed, overestimating their importance, and underestimating the ability of God to speak for Godself. Perhaps saddest of all, many Christians have lost connection with the mystical roots of their own tradition of faith. The church in the third century was much better equipped to find common ground with other spiritual pilgrims than we are in the late twentieth.

The search in these pages is not for safeguards. The religious arena in Aotearoa New Zealand is already well fenced, with locks on all the gates and full security alarms around the perimeter. What we look for here is some common, open ground for everyone curious about spirituality in Aotearoa New Zealand who wonders how and where the Kiwi Spirit is moving in our midst.

But, you say, what do you mean by Kiwi Spirit? Aren't you talking about something that really belongs to yacht races and test matches, and is best sponsored by banks and breweries? Yet that is precisely where most interest to date has been shown in the Kiwi Spirit, and that's the tragedy — that the religious community has been unable or unwilling to connect its traditions and knowledge of 'spirit' with what is happening out in the marketplace and on the playing field. In that vacuum of serious dialogue, spirit becomes a commercialised, secular concept divorced from any spiritual heritage. And then we wonder why young people keep their distance from churches, temples and synagogues.

It's nothing to do with a lack of interest in spirituality. According to a 1991 Massey University survey, 70 percent of New Zealanders believe somehow in a God, yet only a fraction of that number, less than 15 percent, are committed to any religious institution.

The other great fear that inhibits our exploration of the Kiwi Spirit is that knee-jerk charge of pantheism that has been levelled since the missionaries from Europe first arrived and sought to replace the Maori spiritual universe with a 'Christian' one. Figures like Thomas Kendall, who moved from his fundamentalist evangelical origins to embrace a theology that respected cultural differences, were harshly condemned. The charges of pagan superstition linger on, forcing Maori Christians to make impossible and destructive choices between culture and faith. The fear of identifying God too closely with creation has spilled over into Pakeha life and the effect has been to delay any understanding or enjoyment of the created world as the theatre of God's indiscriminate and often playful presence.

Spirituality, then, is the sleeper topic of our life and times. Almost totally ignored by our media, carefully avoided in public by our politicians, caricatured by our advertising industry, it continues to provoke intense curiosity among old and young alike. This book offers some new handles on a conversation that's going on all round us but is so hard to decipher because the old religious vocabulary simply doesn't engage or explain any more.

So, with the greatest respect to all our religious traditions, let's try to stand back from their words for a while, in an attempt to see and hear what the Spirit is saying in this time and place. It's a task I can attempt only because of the confidence my own tradition has given me.

In this search for a Kiwi spirituality there are some old words that

I can't find substitutes for – the word God, for example, in its masculine or feminine (Godde) form. It remains an amazingly resilient description of that source of love and life which lies at the heart of the universe and in whom we live and move and have our being.

Then there is the concept of 'soul', which is fundamental to this search. Again, it's impossible to define precisely. The most recent and most popular attempt at an explanation was made by Thomas Moore in his book, *Care of the Soul*. He sees the soul not as a thing but as a dimension of experiencing our life and ourselves; a dimension that lies somewhere between understanding and the unconscious. Its chief instrument is the imagination, it has to do with genuineness and depth, and, says Moore, it's revealed through attachment, love and community. You know the soul as much by its absence as its presence. When it's not cared for, this shows up in obsession, violence and loss of meaning.

Spirituality, then, is the art and craft of nurturing this soul that we all have and must care for in order to be whole people. Spirituality is in no way the preserve of the religious or the good and the pious. It's a condition of being fully human that is pursued in the secular world, as well as the sacred. New Zealand Roman Catholic theologian Neil Darragh's recent definition says it most succinctly: spirituality is the whole 'combination of beliefs and practices which animate and integrate people's lives'.

All the classical definitions of spirituality contain this theme of integration and wholeness: 'the lived connection of body, mind and spirit', 'the harmony of all that is within and without', 'the gathered response of a whole life to the inner call of God', 'the capacity to go out and beyond oneself . . . in order to respond openly to God', living in and seeing the world in such a way that 'all that takes place becomes part of the mystery of God's life with us'. The part of us which recognises that unfolding mystery is the soul.

In Moore's definition of the soul, one sentence intrigues me and connects with much of what this book is about: 'When you look closely at the image of soulfulness, you see that it is tied to life in all its particulars – good food, satisfying conversation, genuine friends, and experiences that stay in the memory and touch the heart'. Our search for a Kiwi spirituality, if we are to take Moore's words seriously, has to be grounded in concrete realities rather than abstractions, in ordinary, everyday things and events that belong in everyone's experience, not only that of the more holy and worthy among us.

But why a 'Kiwi' spirituality? Surely that's too parochial, even if we could ever agree on what it means? One obvious feature of any spirituality is that it is never second-hand. Each one of us, in every culture, at every time in history, discovers the divine spirit, the sense of the holy afresh, for the first time. There are historical, psychological and theological connections between my experience of the Spirit now in Aotearoa and someone else's at another time and place. But what happens here is original. The Jews never had any doubt about that. Nor did the writers of any of the sacred texts that shape our faiths.

I am convinced that our hesitation about a distinctive Kiwi spirituality is as much about our scepticism over whether there is a distinctive Kiwi identity for any dimension of our life here, spiritual or not. We happily allow such a distinctiveness for the way we play rugby, shear sheep and cook pavlovas, but when it comes to more substantial features of our common life, our confidence in what 'Kiwi' means subsides. Attach the word to Spirit and a hundred devout Christians will stand up and tell you all the bad things about life here and the dangers of encouraging demons.

This book argues that our anxiety is misplaced and that we have more than enough that is genuine and deep around which we can build a unique spirituality. What's more, all the good qualities about life here – the manageable size, the modesty of our manners and lifestyle, the beauty of the natural landscape, the heritage of a treaty that lets us all live here with dignity, the history of spending more time talking to than killing each other – can help us to create a spirituality of our own that will fit our landscape and our humanity. And that is as good a way as any to keep the demons of excessiveness and greed under control. Devils, after all, hate to be subjected to proportion and balance and harmony – the qualities that make for beautiful things.

We're talking about a unique Spirit, never an exclusive one. If it is the Spirit of God that speaks to us through our Kiwi experience, then that's something to share with all the world. It doesn't belong to us; it's simply a gift that fell on our heads, into our hands, in this time and place.

Although I write as a Pakeha, I have deliberately used the word 'Kiwi' more often because it's the most neutral adjective on offer, given the debate that rages about cultural identity in Aotearoa New Zealand. Although my use of Kiwi is weighted in favour of Pakeha culture, it still has the advantage of painting the picture with a broader brush. It clearly acknowledges interaction with Maori. It doesn't pretend to prescribe or define, as the word Pakeha does, and, because it is used more in popular culture than in academia, it takes itself less seriously. This is a book that offers impressions rather than analysis, pieces that need to be fitted into a much larger mosaic of cultural identity. And if the word Kiwi is still helpful for that task, let's use it. Kiwiana, after all, is symbolised by the Buzzy Bee, a children's toy! Not a bad symbol to begin with when you're dealing with a topic like spirituality, which so easily tips us into becoming too earnest and serious for our own good.

CHAPTER 1

Spirituality's fine, subscribe to mine

Discussion of spirituality carries no exemption from the screw-ups and silliness that we meet in every other part of our lives. And, in the superheated climate of Kiwi sensitivity about anything to do with race, gender and identity, spirituality is an especially loaded topic – bent, shoved and grabbed at as never before.

It's an open season subject. Nobody has a corner on the market. No one has a ready-made, all-purpose brand of spirituality for every Kiwi occasion. So everybody has their own version.

Television New Zealand promotes a self-congratulatory, bright and positive no-matter-what-because-together-we're-one kind of spirituality. It takes care not to link itself with the images of any organised religion, while still promoting a sense of mystery, universal value and endless possibility. Lotto has established a variation of its own. The spirituality here relies on images of intense community, embracing all cultures and age groups. Life in Lotto Land is one long party, with everyone enjoying themselves. The bright advertising colours point to the unrelenting optimism. The power of positive thinking and the attraction of partytime overwhelm the one in 7000-year odds against winning the major prize.

There are a hundred other equally distinctive and powerful name brand spiritualities spawned by the consumer culture. They shamelessly exploit images of eternity, mystery, abiding value, nature mysticism, true love, warm community. They claim the blessing of heritage and aristocratic class and pick up trimmings of culture, art, music and design from around the world. These spiritualities sell us things by making us feel good, included and important. They offer immediate satisfaction and inspiration with the least possible pain and cost, and provide only the barest information necessary to achieve the desired effect, glossing over anything inconvenient, ugly or unpleasant.

Above all else, they offer us security and peace of mind. Anything surprising or unmanageable is firmly distanced.

These spiritualities of consumerism are far more powerful than the old-fashioned creeds of atheism and Satanism that religious leaders target as the enemy. Swastikas and burning crosses make colourful opposition but, in Aotearoa New Zealand, there are more fundamental obstacles in the way of a fully human Kiwi spirituality.

The strongest opposition comes from those who say that the realm of the spirit is an optional extra for building community, shaping the economy, finding models of health and wholeness: the cost accountants who have no column on their spreadsheets for this thing called Kiwi Spirit; the politicians who invoke it in their speeches but whose only real allegiance is to the mysteries of free-market competition; and the media marketers who use the language of spirituality to insulate us from reality rather than open us to each other and the world as it is. All these people prosper because Kiwi spirituality is so easily co-opted and abused, cheap and easy for the highest bidder.

Is it possible, then, to sketch a list of the best qualities that define the Kiwi Spirit, and the spirituality that promotes it? However tentative and cloudy such a profile might be, it's worth attempting, because, in the absence of any wider consensus, Saatchi & Saatchi, the Business Roundtable, TVNZ and any number of political parties are already in the business of defining Kiwi spirituality for us, unasked.

My list of defining features for a healthy Kiwi spirituality would include:

- commitment to finding wholeness and integration of different interests;
- engagement with the world as it is, rather than some fanciful version of how it might be or once was;
- desire for growth toward a richer and fuller humanity, beyond any form of dependency, reaching out for *life* in all its fullness;
- respect for the diversity of people as they are and the beliefs they hold;
- willingness to be accountable to a community rather than working in isolation;

- freedom from coercion, bullying and manipulation;
- commitment to seek justice and give respect for all, regardless of gender, race or creed, and to resist anything that distorts or diminishes the dignity of every person;
- respect for the goodness, beauty and fragility of all creation;
- trust that the place and the peoples of Aotearoa New Zealand here and now are as important a venue and channel for the mystery of God as any other place and time.

It's a hugely ambitious list, I know, but it is a minimal one, pretending in no way to be an adequate description of any particular tradition of spirituality. The purpose of this exercise is not to be prescriptive, but simply to find some starting point and common ground for a still emerging Kiwi spirituality. And in a country where the traditional guardians of things spiritual have been better known for building barbed wire fences than for opening gates, a modest goal like finding common ground is still a large ambition. This is not an exercise in defining some new orthodoxy that guarantees the Kiwi Spirit will always be the Holy Spirit of a Trinitarian God; that's a wider search, not attempted here. This is an endeavour to find some soulmates outside the circle of the like-minded and already converted, and to begin a conversation on a topic in which everyone has a stake and about which hardly anybody will speak out loud.

Unlike many traditional cultures, where a distinctive spirituality is embedded in the landscape and the psyche, Pakeha New Zealanders are still learning to trust that our experience contains any sort of original or important spiritual dimension at all. The days are gone when any one religious tradition or denomination could attempt that task of spiritual discovery alone or over against another.

It is naive to talk about a Kiwi spirituality without some consensus about what it's for. But even a list half as long as the one I suggest would help in giving each other confidence that we already hold something in common that is distinctive and precious and strong enough to resist all the efforts to short-change or sell it off.

Chapter 2

No religion, please, we're spiritual – the boundaries between sacred and secular

It's no surprise that a recent survey showed New Zealand to be among the most secular countries in the Western world, most suspicious of anything officially religious. You can get away with telling New Zealanders they are all on board an America's Cup yacht, or part of an All Black team. But telling them that they should all be at church on Sunday is about as useful as shouting out the window.

In New Zealand, talking in public about religion is an unfashionable thing to do. National Radio, as a public broadcaster, might be expected to be the exception, but even this worthy enterprise has reduced its coverage of matters spiritual from 1.85 to 1.09 percent of its total output. Percentage points that low become meaningless.

So, by the end of the century in Aotearoa New Zealand, we are missing any seriously informed and systematic media coverage of religious, spiritual or church-related issues. They simply don't rate as newsworthy. Garden compost gets better coverage.

New Zealand is peculiar in this regard. In the United States, religion still makes major news. Newspapers like the *Dallas Morning News* devote a whole weekend section to the subject. In Western Europe, specialist reporters and editors cover religion across all the media, even where churchgoing is unpopular. There's some knowledge and background, even if there isn't much sympathy.

Not so here. When religious angles to news stories do arise, New Zealand editors display a dismal lack of background, balance and the most elementary information.

So the Presbyterian Assembly's negative decision on ordaining gay and lesbian people was treated by mainstream media as though it were a strange, isolated event affecting one church, rather than a major news story currently being repeated, with interesting variations, in all churches across the United States, Canada, Brazil, Western Europe and Britain.

When the dramatisation of Joanna Trollope's novel, *The Choir*, was screened here, there was no television curiosity about whether the same story might be sitting on our own doorstep, which it was – under our own steeples. There were three or four equally turbulent stories of choral disharmony, Kiwi style, that could have been told at the time. Much to the relief of the churches concerned, no one was interested.

The Vicar of Dibley won good TV audience ratings for a while. More surprisingly, so did *Father Ted*. But there are a dozen New Zealand priests, male and female, whose slapstick skills and real-life stories would make better television with a little help from your broadcasting fee.

Religion has never been tackled by any New Zealand film or television series and its days on radio are numbered. Yet, despite this, the exploration of Kiwi spirituality is the strongest single theme of all media coverage, both in the advertising commercials and the programmes between them. So long as religion isn't mentioned explicitly, churches don't appear and clergy are portrayed as clowns, spiritual issues can be freely discussed. So soap operas explore the meaning of life, current affairs weigh issues of life and death, drama series map the human heart, and the news on the hour tells us what it means to be human now. And our media gatekeepers see nothing contradictory about any of this. Spirituality is acceptable. Religion is not.

The tragedy is that the stories which do involve religious traditions and communities of faith are constantly forgotten or distorted by lack of context and understanding, and mislead and miss the point. They end up painting Ireland's problems as arising from a simple confrontation between Catholic and Protestant, which they don't. They describe New Zealand's carefully focused Christian Heritage Party in a media shorthand that makes it seem to represent all Christians, which it doesn't. They deal with issues of sexuality as purely modern, purely moral dilemmas, which they aren't. They paint treaty issues as purely political grievances rather than breaches of a spiritual covenant, which they are, and they portray the Crusades as a romantic medieval adventure that makes entertaining late-evening television, rather than a religious mindset with a dangerous history that is very much alive and well in New Zealand.

What is worse, our church-, synagogue- and temple-shy media miss some marvellous stories of New Zealanders who, because of their faith, are working for restorative justice, dealing with personal crisis, discovering healing available nowhere else, coping with cultural diversity in ways that the secular community might like to know about as well. As a consequence, these stories remain this country's best kept secrets.

Holy is an ambiguous word in the Kiwi vocabulary. Just what does this word mean? You could start with a vision like the one you read about in the prophet Isaiah – winged angels in a smoke-filled temple, an experience of God so overwhelming that it is etched on our imagination forever. Two and a half thousand years later, despite its quaint, outlandish images, it still speaks to us.

Theologians ever since have tried to find words to explain such visions: mystery, otherness, the numinous, the supernatural, the space beyond our understanding. Ironically enough, it is now the scientific community that leads the search for these new words. Atomic physicists and mathematicians and astronomers who speculate on the worlds beyond the black holes in the universe help us to reimage what we mean by holy.

The boundaries of sacred and secular keep shifting on us. Theology used to be the most secure and fixed of disciplines. Now it is the most fluid, the easiest in which to get lost and left behind, if you let your understanding of what is sacred or secular stand still.

The word secular keeps changing too. Literally, it means a focus on this age, the here and now. It needn't be the dirty word that some politicians and church leaders make it out to be. If the secular is all we have to say and all there is to see, we're in trouble. But if the secular can't be the place to start when we celebrate God's presence, infinitely wider though that presence may be, then the boundary riders have got it wrong. The divisions between the secular and the sacred need to be constantly revised.

The New Testament is full of stories of such revisions. Jesus spent his time challenging the boundaries around holy times and places. He taught from fishing boats and hillsides as well as in temples (in fact, he was thrown out of some temples), and he challenged that most holy institution of the day, the Sabbath, claiming that it was made for people and not vice versa.

The lines we draw around the sacred and the secular may be useful for our culture and tradition. They may give us the security and continuity we sometimes need. But they are only the most approximate of guides for finding how and where God is present and active in our lives. And when we take these boundaries too seriously, God delights in turning them inside out and upside down.

Another way of putting this is to talk of the hiddenness of God, as theologian Carl Michalson has done: 'It is God's way of life to be hidden'. Not to be tied to guaranteed appearances in the holy places of our choice, doing the sacred things that suit us, but hidden in our lives – in human actions of justice, mercy and love; in the beauty of the natural world; and modelled for all time by the one who came to live in our midst, like us in every way, full of grace and truth.

At the Anglican Church's General Synod in Rotorua in 1996, the three tikanga (cultural pathways), Maori, Pakeha and Polynesian, met to try to work out where God was leading them for the next two years. There were lots of services of worship and speeches and sermons – it's hard to hear the difference at meetings like this. But the moments when the leading of the Spirit of God was clearest didn't come at the holy times or in the sacred places. The Spirit was most evident when people who had lost their confidence and their gifts, rediscovered their voice and their future. When those things happened, a new kind of unity was experienced between cultures, and between women and men, across all the old divisions of secular and sacred.

On a Sunday night in Rotorua, the synod met for a meal on the marae at Ohinemutu, after some bruising debates between the tikanga over issues of precedence and money and power. There were sermons and prayers to heal the wounds but, for me, the healing was most evident when a singer stood up, and spontaneously moved among the delegates in the hall, even the ones who were finding it difficult to talk to each other.

There was nothing religious about this, and the song she led, *Won't You Come Home, Bill Bailey*, wasn't very sacred at all. Secular stuff but, on that Sunday night, it proved to be a channel of healing and grace. And the energy that people found in singing that song together carried them into and through a difficult week.

When we learn to stop worrying about the boundaries between secular and sacred, it becomes easier to see where the Spirit of God is moving in our midst. When we can stop fencing God in with these boundaries we create, God liberates us in unimaginable ways and the discovery of a Kiwi spirituality becomes much easier.

Spiritual feelings and values are valued, even fashionable, but to name them or associate them with religion is to move on to dangerous ground. Any suggestion that spirituality is best nourished within that tradition or this lifestyle draws suspicion and hostility. It's as though we believe you can have a spiritual life without giving it a name or providing a discipline to nurture it. True spirituality takes care of itself.

The reality is more complicated and in order to explore it we need to reclaim some of these discredited words, such as piety, for example. It simply means to make what you believe in visible and tangible. The original Latin word meant giving respect to one's ancestors, but we use it more broadly to include our spiritual allegiances and values which, in Pakeha society, we don't always share with our ancestors. Piety, by definition, must be demonstrated and shown. It must wear a face, find a form, create a culture. That's what piety means and, until we find a better word, we'll have to make do with it.

One way of lowering distaste for the word is to recognise the many different ways in which piety is expressed. Traditionally we've focused on language, manner and behaviour. To call someone pious is to label the way they speak and act, but it can equally well include the way people dress and eat, the way they rear children, drive cars, organise their social lives and just about any other activity through which we demonstrate our values and loyalties. The bone carvings worn around our necks, the fashion currency of our hairstyles, kitchen appliances and garment labels all speak as loudly of our piety as the frequency of our church attendance or the absence of four-letter expletives in our vocabulary. The place where we choose to live, the car we choose to drive, the kind of parties we attend all speak volumes about our piety – whether it is modest and respectful of others or righteous and smug, whether it exhibits a brand of goodness (or badness) that is worn easily or rubbed in your face. Piety is expressed in an endless variety of ways and with a limitless subtlety of expression.

In Kiwi culture, piety is judged with a particular savagery. The current obsession with political correctness is another version of our national inability to handle our pieties with ease and grace. So we campaign for inclusive language, gender equity, racial equality, ecological respect with a zeal that leaves the offenders feeling dirty and the campaigners shining clean and bright.

The reasons for this characteristic overkill are bound up with the curious mixture of secular government and sectarian rivalry in early Pakeha settlement, long-standing hostility to any institutional form of religion, the legacy of moralistic, world-denying theology, the reluctance of churches to wean themselves from their colonial dependencies – English, Irish or Scottish denominationalism and later American-style revivalism.

The hardest thing of all to find are people who wear their spiritual convictions with confidence and ease. The stereotype that New Zealanders most love to hate is that of a 'religious' person whose high-mindedness is contradicted by a pathetic personality and a misplaced zeal for converting others. To be spiritual is to be intense and earnest. Anything spiritual is reserved for nice (and slightly wet) people. Nothing has done more to stunt the growth of Kiwi spirituality.

Back in 1883, the *New Zealand Herald* reported on a revival service in the Mangere Presbyterian Church. 'The assemblage was a tolerably fair one,' wrote the journalist. 'It seemed fairly attentive and made up of old and young people of both sexes. Both the reverend gentlemen leading the service appeared to be decidedly in earnest.'

That summed up the occasion. The caricature of matters religious was already in place and we've been pouring more cement into this mould ever since. Anything in a lighter vein or a different rhythm doesn't fit.

In 1995, the director of the television series *Heartland*, usually eager for adventurous and original facets of New Zealand life, proved curiously reluctant to mention the Christchurch Cathedral's jazz services in a programme on the city fronted by Gary McCormick. All mention of these services and anything else in the cathedral's repertoire that didn't fit the traditional stereotype of earnest, old-fashioned religion was left out of the episode that went to air, including an interview that explained the range of new cathedral initiatives on offer.

When challenged, the director explained to me: 'I filmed [your] interview in good faith and was interested in what you had to say… although privately I appreciated the cathedral more as a valuable link to values and attitudes of those who had come before me, than as a venue for jazz. In the event, however, it was quite a difficult concept to get across, and it was impossible to justify the time required to present the issue of the cathedral's changing image. To explain your aims in that regard… would have caused an unsightly bulge in the film. I realise that the whole question is not at all marginal to you, but my priorities are necessarily those of prime time television.'

When the makers and gatekeepers of 'quality' television are so committed to preserving such traditional (and, in my view, negative) piety, the chances of changing these stereotypes look daunting. The effect is to keep spirituality as a marginal, private activity, imprisoned in forms of piety that do no justice to our experience here and now.

Piety, or a new word that means the same thing, needs to be reclaimed and restored to include the full range of expressing our spiritual values and visions. The guardians of the old piety, whether they stand in churches or in television production houses, need to stand back and let go. A new generation of Kiwi musicians and artists are singing and painting spiritual messages easily and unashamedly, with a breadth and depth unheard of a decade ago. Piety isn't a word that belongs in the vocabulary of this new generation, but pious is what they are, in the full sense of that word. Until the word is owned by everyone who respects the spiritual dimension of life, regardless of how orthodox or alternative they might be, the search for an authentic Kiwi spirituality is going to be diverted and derailed.

A generous acceptance of and respect for each other's piety is a fundamental first step in giving spirituality a proper place in Kiwi culture, and ensuring that our children enjoy the legacy of spiritual values we have inherited. In traditional societies, that legacy is handed on by rites of passage and daily rituals to mark our going and coming, our meals, our meetings, our waking and going to sleep. Pakeha culture has given up most of these rituals of acknowledgement and gratitude for the holiness of ordinary life. Such natural and unconscious expressions of piety have to be reclaimed or replaced with other forms that give our children the message that spiritual allegiances and interests are as normal as watching television or eating hamburgers.

⊱┄◈┄◉┄◈┄⊰

Kiwi culture is rough, too, on any group that even smells of altruism and public goodness. The label 'do gooder' is intended as a wounding insult, carrying with it an often unspoken distrust of personal motivation and an expectation that the person in question is probably a wowser as well. The caricaturing endured by the Women's Christian Temperance Union in the late nineteenth century still shocks today. Their success in helping to win the vote for women served only to fuel the attacks and perpetuate the stereotype that spirituality is really a women's domain.

In the traditional, largely male Kiwi view, goodness and kindness, worthiness and politeness are all qualities embraced by the blanket term 'nice'. And that, above all other qualities, is a precondition for anything even vaguely to do with spirituality. It helps to explain why religious causes and institutions in this country are overwhelmingly female in their membership and culture, even though the balance of leadership and structural power is still held and exercised by men.

The curse of niceness runs deep. For a start, it short-changes the reality of the way things are, holding up a Pollyanna version in which people smile more than is convincing and life seems to go more smoothly than we have ever experienced it. Kim Hill, on her morning session on National Radio, has complained about the 'relentless cheerfulness' of the current diet of television programmes. The mixture of sitcoms, game shows and home-grown lifestyle episodes all conspire to convince us that everyone is happy, photogenic and having a ball.

As well as begging questions and contradictions, the cult of niceness smoothes out all the subtleties of Kiwi culture and disconnects us from the energy and excitement that life can offer when we take it as it is, the nice and the nasty together. For it's behind some of the roughest and most unlikely exteriors that we find the gems of Kiwi spirituality. The unsung saints who care for severely disabled people, who keep voluntary unpaid and unthanked community services going, who work harder and longer than they need to in jobs that are dangerous and dirtier and more arduous than most of us would put up with – many of these people are not 'nice' much of the time. They don't fit any of the stereotypes and they don't use any of the predictable language yet their spirituality of perseverance and sacrifice and ungrudging service is inspirational. Our obsession with niceness as a precondition for spiritual value means these people are ignored and overlooked.

Far from being a precondition, niceness is an obstacle to be destroyed in the poetry of James K. Baxter. God, for him, became a stench in the nostrils of nice people and a Kiwi spirituality could only be found as far away as possible from the ordered civility of middle-class life:

Who is harsher than this God of ours? Who is harder to love or be loved by? The God they imagine, and pray to very often in the churches, is a God of sugar compared to the terrible One who grips our living entrails, who drives both good and evil from our souls, as if both were his enemies, and fills us with anguish and darkness. I would not advise any man to follow him. He comes like the sandstorm out of the desert, or the avalanche on a mountain village, or tons of black water from the depths of the sea.

You think he might take away your health or your happiness or your sanity, but he will always leave you your morality. Don't count on it. . .

He may shatter your morality as you yourself step on a snail alongside your doorway. What is our morality to be but God himself?

He turns this man into an old coat and a broken stick. He makes him the nuns' devil and a bad smell in the noses of good churchgoing people. It's not a pleasant vocation.

We may not have to cope with a no-frills commune on the banks of the Whanganui River, full of displaced and desperate young people, but our search for a Kiwi spirituality has to make room for every sort and condition of human experience that Aotearoa New Zealand has to offer. We're as likely to find the wisdom we need in the darker, messier, forgotten corners of our culture. The anxious streets of South Auckland or the isolation of West Coast bush – these provide fertile ground for the Kiwi Spirit. Wherever men and women are working hard to survive, questioning the way things are, reframing their lives, struggling to start over again, making room for people and ideas they once couldn't cope with, there the Kiwi Spirit may well be seen and heard.

Spirituality, after all, is about something as unpredictable as the wind, as subtle and hard to see as breathing. The old Hebrew word for spirit translates as divine breath. How ironic that we've allowed something so universal and elusive, so surprising and mysterious, to become confined only to nice people in nice places.

Chapter 3

Lamps on
– is the Spirit moving?

The feature I liked most in my 1985 Ford Falcon ute wasn't the throb of its 4.1-litre motor, although that was very nice, or the strength of its reinforced back springs, although that was very reassuring when you were overloaded on a wet night. What I enjoyed most was a simple little red dashboard light that read 'lamps on'. Without any assistance from the driver, it told you when your headlights were on or off. That was very helpful, especially at twilight, or under competition from bright streetlights.

When you came to the end of a lukewarm day, full of meetings that went nowhere and issues that went round and round and people who were neither hot nor cold, then it was good to get into the truck and drive away with the dashboard lit up and the sign that said 'lamps on' glowing in the dark.

I wish it were as easy to know when the Spirit was moving. I wish there were a 'lamps on' sign somewhere I could turn to. I wish I knew how to switch on such a sign myself.

Sometimes I think I do, especially when I hear songs that I love, although when I sing those same songs myself in the shower, then the feeling isn't the same, not by a country mile. I can sometimes feel the Spirit moving when I walk on the beach or watch the sun go down over a bush-clad valley and see the colours change from green to deepest blue to black. In the eyes of a child and the courage of a cancer patient who can still smile and in the inspiration of some filmmakers, I can feel the Spirit moving. Yet all those people and circumstances can also fill me with great despair, and the feelings run empty and turn sour.

There's another test of whether the Spirit is moving. There might not be a 'lamps on' sign on hand but you can look and see if the lights are burning. According to this test, you will know because it glows. There are plenty of examples – the pillar of fire that the people of Israel remember they saw in the desert, or the tongues of fire that they saw descending in Jerusalem, or a thousand visions that people of faith have experienced down the ages. When the Bible talks about the glory of God, it literally means the radiance of God, God's ability to glow and be seen, with such an intensity of light that it dazzles your eyes and bleaches your clothes.

That's a wonderful metaphor, but it's been spoiled for anyone who has watched the special effects in too many movies about close encounters of every conceivable kind. 'You know because it glows' is a sure-fire strategy for anyone with a little money and a few extra candlepower. And the brighter you can make the glow, the more certain you can make your audience.

Another favourite test of whether the Spirit really is moving is to ask how different your experience is. Is it really and truly different and quite, quite special? According to this approach, anything familiar and ordinary and everyday is probably not the real thing. And anything that's been around for a while is probably worn out. God is either doing a new thing or not doing anything at all.

That's a very contemporary approach to testing the Spirit. It fits perfectly with the philosophy of the six o'clock news. If you've seen it before, it isn't worth repeating.

But this Spirit we're talking about has been around since the first day of creation. The Spirit of God is the very breath of God that brought the world into being and has been the source of life ever since. All the different expressions of that Spirit throughout history connect back into that divine energy present since the world began. And that same Spirit is driving ahead of us into the future till the end of the world, catching up every living thing in the birth pangs of a liberation that we can only dream about.

Strong stuff, but ordinary stuff, in the sense that this Spirit is everywhere about us. It is the part of God that keeps us living and loving and hoping and longing for the truth to be told. Making the connections between us and others, with the world and with God – the go-between God. Incorporating, anchoring, earthing, including. That's what the Spirit does.

And we experience that Spirit inside our skins, with our feet on the ground, constrained by time and money and the weather and the traffic conditions, and what we had for dinner (if we had dinner), and what makes it worth getting up tomorrow morning – all the dismay and the delight of living in Aotearoa New Zealand. The Kiwi Spirit connects us with the universal Spirit, everything in which we live and move and have our being, here and now. Hildegaard of Bingen said it best, 700 years ago:

> The Holy Spirit is life that gives life,
> Moving all things.
> It is the root in every creature
> And purifies all things.
> Wiping away sins, anointing wounds.
> It is radiant life, worthy of praise,
> Awakening and enlivening all things.

That's the realm of the Spirit of God. Keep looking overseas or across Cook Strait or up in the sky or over your shoulder and you'll miss the Spirit that is always closer than you think; closer and more ordinary.

The hunger for something extraordinary keeps getting in the way. Looking for a Spirit that is extraordinary and new and different is a bit like waiting for the security of a dashboard light to tell you what's going on outside. But you can't test the Spirit like that. It's wider and deeper than any technology could ever measure, always beyond our control. James K. Baxter said it eloquently, in words that are used in *A New Zealand Prayer Book*:

> Holy Spirit,
> You blow like the wind in a thousand paddocks,
> Inside and outside the fences,
> You blow where you wish to blow.

What we can be sure of is that the Spirit is a gift, given to us whether or not we're deserving or worthy or ready. It's the gift of life itself, of hope and faith and trust and everything that keeps us going.

St Paul explains it in a wonderful sentence he wrote to the people of Corinth. 'What do you have that you didn't receive?' What can you claim about your life that wasn't given to you?

That doesn't help us understand why the gifts seem to be so unfairly distributed at times; why it is that some people manage to drive utes not only with dashboard lights but also with power steering and central locking and Dolby sound. But it does remind us that we brought nothing into the world and take nothing out; that everything we enjoy is a gift from God, given through the Spirit of God.

The interest in spirituality in our time is unbounded. Everywhere you see the signs of people hungering for something deeper, richer, that will connect and include and affirm them with each other and the universe. The news that there might have been, might still be, life on Mars sends the world into a frenzy of excitement and uncertainty and calls for a coast-to-coast broadcast by President Clinton.

And such confusion. If you see and feel for certain that the Spirit is moving, if it feels good and glows well, then it must be true. But that might be the most unreliable evidence of all. Ask, instead, whether this Spirit you feel and see, even if only as a hint and a glimpse, is with you in the ordinary and everyday; whether it's liberating and turning you outwards to join with others and connect with the world.

And, most of all, ask yourself whether this Spirit is helping us see that everything we have we have been given; that our very life and breath, to say nothing of our hope and our future, are as much a gift as the music that we hear and the air we breathe. When we start to see the Spirit in these ways, then we don't have to fret about where the Spirit is and isn't to be found. Everywhere we tread becomes holy ground. Every breath we take. Every song we sing. We don't need the security of a dashboard light to say that the lamps are on. They're burning all the time.

CHAPTER 4

Not just poppies
– the Anzac Spirit

This creature called Kiwi spirituality is so elusive that we need to catch bits of it by surprise. Anniversaries are a great time for sneaking up on it as it lies there sunning itself on a war memorial, in the middle of a crowd, or in the hall afterwards over a cup of tea. It doesn't matter too much if it's not your anniversary and you never fought the battle or attended the school being remembered. In some ways, it's an advantage not to stand too close. All that matters is that the event remembered is anchored in the experience of enough New Zealanders and is drenched in enough tears and laughter. We learn more about the spirituality we share through studying these snapshots of our heritage than we do from a hundred desperate attempts to pin down where the Kiwi Spirit is moving now.

The value of anniversaries is being rediscovered by new generations of New Zealanders. The revival of interest in Anzac Day is a case in point. Generations born long after all the wars now attend the services and listen to the reveille and the last post. These rituals speak to the newcomers not of parade grounds and army camps they've never seen, but of the romance of soldiering woven into family stories, of fighting for forgotten causes in impossibly foreign places, of defending ideals that bemuse us now in an age where patriotism is hard to spell.

The memories that anniversaries trigger can still excite. When VJ Day was marked fifty years after the end of the Second World War, they tracked down a sailor who kissed a woman he'd never met in the Times Square crowd in New York on that day in 1945. The picture of that kiss had been immortalised but the couple remained anonymous until they were reunited on television and talked about their amorous encounter as if it had happened yesterday. It was really a very proper sort of kiss, wasn't it, said the sailor, with the benefit of half a century of hindsight. And the woman smiled.

The first VJ Day in New Zealand was no less exciting, if the pictures and newspaper prose of the time are any indication. Lots of people did outrageous things together. Lots of usually restrained editorial writers wrote words like these: 'Japan has today surrendered. The last of our enemies is laid low. This is it. This is the day. It was expected but it was still a surprise – a grand, glorious, never to be forgotten surprise. Japan has surrendered. Magnificent, earth circling news, news so momentous that it wrenched workmen from their benches, children from their school desks, and uplifted mothers and housewives from their home labours.' You could still write like that back in 1945. 'Let them ring, let them hoot, let them scream – loudly, continuously – those sirens of joy. And let voices join them. The war is over.'

Fifty years on, we savour the joy and the relief of that moment again. But it was a poignant moment too, on that first VJ Day, because they hadn't been able to weigh up the full cost of the war: the 12,000 dead New Zealanders, the thousands more maimed and scarred by visible wounds and invisible nightmares, the relationships that could never be rebuilt, the gaps in families that could never be filled again. And they didn't have the casualty figures from Hiroshima and Nagasaki: 150,000 killed in fractions of a second and thousands more subject to an eternity of radioactive slow poison.

They didn't know all that back in 1945. It was enough to know that the most horrific war the world had ever known had finally ended. But now, with a new generation and a new century ahead of us, we must do more than remember. We must make sense of what's happened to us since that first VJ Day.

Imagine the reaction if you had told those cheering crowds in 1945 that Japan would become a major player in our economy, fill our churches with tourists, own large chunks of our city shops and our countryside, supply nearly all our cars and run TV ads that welcome us to our world.

And imagine the reaction of the crowd if we told them that the bomb which destroyed Hiroshima and Nagasaki would dominate the imagination and the anxiety of the world as nothing else before it, that it would create a story of environmental terror and destruction, become the pivot point of international politics for half a century and a central issue for every Pacific nation within sailing distance of Moruroa. Imagine if they knew, back in 1945, that the politics of resistance to the nuclear industry would shape our national identity from the 1970s and an accompanying defiant, clean, green spirituality that has been developing ever since.

But it's still hard to make sense of what's happened since 1945, especially if your family and community have carried the cost of the war in personal terms. You look at those grotesquely long lists of the dead on the war memorials of little provincial towns, lists so long that you wonder who was left, and you have to ask about the point of it all, and who the winners and the losers really are. It's very easy to get locked into cycles of bitterness and regret. It's still very hard for some to forgive and it's quite impossible, on VJ Day or Anzac Day, to ask people to forget.

The Book of Job gives us some help in the midst of our remembering and our wondering. When Job is faced with similar contradictions and mysteries too great to explain, God suggests that he change his frame of reference. Where were you, God asks, when I laid the foundations of the earth and set the universe in motion? Break out of the picture frame of your own experience. Reframe your world, remembering that it's the world I made to be good and beautiful and full of peace and promise.

So, apart from marking the end of a war, what else can we celebrate on anniversaries like VJ Day and Anzac Day? In fact, there's plenty to celebrate, for all of us. Our Kiwi spirituality was forged in these wartime experiences, which showed us a long list of national qualities that we didn't know we had. For example, we discovered a sense of pride and independence as a South Pacific people, not living at the far end of an old European world, but rather in the middle of a new Pacific one. We developed an awareness of depths of courage and sacrifice and service that surprised people then and are still treasured today. Those names on the memorials are carved with pride, and are not forgotten.

We learnt, too, that science cannot save us, and that the bomb, which many argue brought peace, will destroy us all if we don't constrain our technology with international diplomacy and alternatives to the arms race. We found a new sense of our interdependence as cultures and nations, especially small island nations – that we are bound together in this bundle of life, and we need each other, even Japanese and New Zealanders, in ways we didn't realise in 1945. And a final, vital feature of this legacy left to us by the experiences recalled on Anzac and VJ Day is our sense of a national identity that depends on all parts of the country, and every culture, making a contribution and being named and heard and seen.

We in Aotearoa New Zealand approach the end of the century with a very tender and fragile understanding of who we are as a nation. We need all the help we can get from symbols and stories that will hold us together and help us to explain to each other who we are – as women and men, Maori and Pakeha, young and old. There are lots of symbols and stories that explain us separately, but very few that require us to address each other, and hold each other accountable.

The Anzac story hasn't always been one that all New Zealanders could claim and make their own. When I grew up with it, in a small East Coast town up north, it was a sacred male story. Only old soldiers went to dawn parades; the memories and the mateship were still too intense to widen the circle. And, in the 1960s, Anzac Day was intensely politicised by the Vietnam War and fights over defence budgets. Politicians used the day to make campaign speeches.

We have used and sometimes abused Anzac Day for all sorts of purposes. It is only in recent times that we have allowed scholars and television producers, even speakers at Anzac Day parades, to start exploring the story critically, openly, in a way that lets all sorts of new people make it their own.

And so we have begun to understand more clearly the sacrifice that women, too, made in those wars – their role, short-lived though it was, not only in uniform, but also at home, in keeping the country going, and their effect on postwar social policy. We have learnt of the traumas that our war heroes have lived with for the rest of their lives, and only recently begun to speak about, as sanitised histories have been replaced. We have discovered how the experience of the Maori Pioneer Battalion in the First War and the 28th Maori Battalion in the Second has shaped race relations in New Zealand and Maori leadership ever since. We have found out something about the treatment of conscientious objectors, 1100 of them, and the mutinies and the riots among not only our prisoners but our own soldiers when they took exception to a military authority that took itself too seriously.

Everything, from the food we eat, to the songs we sing, to the jokes we laugh at, to the times the pubs shut, to attitudes about sexuality, has been shaped by this Anzac story. It is a gold seam of meaning and insight for our search for a national identity and a clearer sense of who we are as New Zealanders.

There's no one place you can go to dig that seam of meaning. Not even Neil Roberts' TV series, *New Zealanders at War*, nor James Belich's *New Zealand Wars*, does that, nor watching Gaylene Preston's movie, *War Stories Our Mothers Never Told Us*. Because so much of this story is between the lines. So much is locked away in the memories of older people who carry the story silently, never having found the words to begin to say what it means, not even to each other. Many of those who fought and served and suffered, abroad and at home, have lost the desire to retell the story because it is too painful, too misused, too long ago. So much of it has become the stuff of legend.

The Anzac story will go on being retold, but with ever greater complication, and imagination, as the stuff that dreams are made of, dreams and nightmares, honouring those who lived it out, and ensuring that those who follow them can make it their own as well.

It seems that this is happening, when you consider the growing attendances at Anzac services and parades. Our identity as peoples of Aotearoa New Zealand is emerging, for both Maori and Pakeha, and the Anzac story is part of that journey, more thoughtfully, with less jingoism and flag waving, than ever before. Increasingly, Anzac is a word that more New Zealanders, young as well as old, can claim. It is a word that acknowledges fear as well as courage, outrage as well as obedience, scepticism as well as idealism, disaster as well as brilliance, horror as well as great beauty. Anzac is no longer a story told to beat the drums of war.

It was war that showed us what we could achieve if we made room for each other. The tragedy is that we've never done so well for the peace effort ever since. The danger is that we'll forget these qualities forged at such cost. Anniversaries like VJ Day and Anzac Day can remind us of this good heritage and the Kiwi Spirit that emerged out of so much suffering. It's a Spirit won at great cost and its roots go way down deep.

Recently, I crossed Cook Strait on the interisland ferry, *Arahura*. Standing on the stern deck, I was surrounded by a crowd of teenagers, watching the wharfies below, dressed in lime-green safety jackets, cast off the lines and winch up the vehicle access ramp. There was no one else on the wharf, no one to see us off on our three-hour voyage. Ferry sailings don't draw crowds in Picton. I knew that so I wasn't disappointed.

But the teenagers around me were. Nobody's here to wave to us, they complained to each other, and the wharfies below didn't seem the least bit interested in obliging, so the teenagers created their own imaginary crowd on the dock. They saw thousands of people cheering and throwing streamers. The kids waved back while the mystified older passengers looked on and we sailed out to sea.

I wouldn't have been able to make much sense out of this little pantomime, had I not seen the movie *Titanic*. I suspect the teenagers around me had seen it several times and bought the CD of the soundtrack and entered their own love affair with Kate Winslet or Leonardo DiCaprio. In less than six months, the movie broke the billion-dollar mark and created a make-believe world of its own, a quaintly Edwardian world of dressing for a twelve-course dinner and keeping the steerage passengers well separated from the upper decks.

Yet today's egalitarian, baggy-panted, sweatshirted, Nike-footed, McDonalds-munching teenagers have been swept away by this film. They come to the horror of this maritime disaster with innocent eyes, free from any personal grief or anger, and enter the story afresh as a wonderful romance. The director, James Cameron, took hold of a tragedy that was rapidly being forgotten and turned it into a love story that everyone will remember, especially everyone under twenty-five.

But although the *Titanic* story will be hard to forget now, even though the last survivors have died, the truth about the sinking will be harder than ever to reach now, behind the photogenic Hollywood version. The families of those who died are reported to feel very ambiguous about the whole affair, especially with the new salvage industry of *Titanic* memorabilia that the film has created.

The Anzac story faces a similar fate. For the day is soon coming when there will be no old soldiers to lead us on Anzac Day, no more medals worn with pride, no more speeches on how it was, no more memories of loved ones who you waved goodbye to at the wharf and who didn't come home. Those experiences, like the *Titanic* saga, will have to be recreated on film and tape with cleverly rearranged images and soundtracks. And that will need to be done with great love and care in case precious parts of the story get left out, in case the ugliness and the horror are glamorised and glossed over, in case the ordinary lives of sacrifice and faithfulness and service are forgotten and only the photogenic heroes in fancy uniforms remain.

The only major movie made about Anzac to date was produced and acted by Australians, which is difficult enough because they are prone to short-term memory loss about the Kiwi part of the Anzac equation. But that will be nothing compared with the inevitable Hollywood treatment of our story and all the other ways that Anzac will be commercialised and marketed and repackaged. Given the disgracefully low proportion of local content on TV, the chances of someone else telling our story for us grows by the day.

The Anzac story of sacrifice and service that is stamped across this Kiwi culture is easily forgotten and readily distorted. The new Museum of New Zealand, Te Papa, dazzling though it is, had hardly any direct acknowledgement of the Anzac story in its opening exhibitions, yet at every point of our nation's story, the Anzac spirit and the Anzac experience have shaped our destiny. Take, for example, the once strong, now shaky resolve to ensure that New Zealand children don't go hungry and old people are honoured and cared for and there are jobs and houses for all. Too many of our soldiers overseas saw too much poverty and sickness, too many hungry children and elderly refugees. They came home determined never to let it happen here.

Our very modern curiosity about who we are as New Zealanders, on which Te Papa is so successfully capitalising, is itself a feature of our Anzac heritage. In those early wars, where the right to fight under our own commanders still had to be won, we had to learn very publicly and very quickly what made us distinctive as New Zealanders.

Like it or not, we are what we remember. Our collective memories shape us as peoples and cultures, just as surely as our personal memories shape our private lives. So how we remember the Anzac story is crucial for all of us, obviously for those who served and ever more so for those who inherit the story. We know that those who forget their history are doomed to repeat it.

So, more than ever before, the Anzac story needs to be held on to and shared around with all the imagination of the *Titanic* movie, and even a little of its money. A country's spirituality doesn't take care of itself. It needs nurturing and promoting, so that new generations are introduced to the stories that carry the Kiwi Spirit. Anzac is one such story.

On the day I sailed on the ferry, the Anzac poppies went on sale in Picton. The teenagers who waved goodbye to the imaginary crowds were all wearing poppies. They had bought them as readily as they bought tickets to *Titanic*. But the poppies were easy for them all to afford. And for their future hope and pride as young New Zealanders, for their spiritual health, the poppies were a much better buy.

Chapter 5

Who do we think we are?
– Maori, Pakeha, Kiwi

To insert a partial word like 'Kiwi' before something as universally worthy as 'spirituality' leaves some of us feeling a little hesitant. Doesn't it reduce the whole subject to a parochial level, making it insular and self-serving? Isn't it just like the way Kiwis behave when they travel overseas to broaden their minds and end up huddled together in one room at Bondi Beach or Earls Court? Isn't what's true of spirituality anywhere true everywhere?

The same questions underlie the current debate on national identity. Can't we all be New Zealanders together and, after that, citizens of the world? Isn't it really a global culture that gives us identity?

The manufacturers of Nike shoes and Hollywood movies love to hear such sentiments, as do the evangelists for the Internet that offers international communication at affordable rates for at least the middle class. For the 70 percent of the world who don't yet have telephones, these invitations are ambiguous at best. Yet even if everyone could afford the Internet, could we leapfrog out of our local identity into a global one? As electronic media and transnational commerce make that possibility a live option, so there are powerful counterforces at work, moving us back to separate grassroots and indigenous identities. Just when technology is making a global culture possible for the first time in history, our distrust of that culture keeps growing and the questions keep nagging – who controls it and benefits from it?

I recently attended a large conference in the United States on the theme of 'global culture and tribal passions', in which the first was portrayed as positive and exciting and the latter as something to be feared and derided. The meeting culminated in a televised discussion interacting with satellite-linked forums across North America. Questions from the studio audience were invited, so I asked, 'What happens if you're not so sure that global culture is a good thing, and that you find lots of good things of the Spirit in so-called "tribal passions"?' Unfortunately, the on-air panel had no time to respond to the question. I still don't know whether they thought it was impolite to ask.

Regardless of how many people get hooked on surfing the Internet or weaving the strands of the World Wide Web, the questions 'Where do you come from?' and 'Where do you live?' remain fundamental in our search for what it is to be human. They are safe questions for inviting personal disclosure, in a way that questions about jobs and marriages no longer are. The questions and answers about place bring us back to where we belong geographically, and the spiritual implications of that physical belonging soon open up.

Cultural anthropologists make a helpful distinction between three sorts of collective identity: the way in which we are like all others, some others and no others. Where we come from and where we live now belong in the 'no others' category and its attraction increases with age. The bond of being hometown boys or girls outlasts most other links, even if you didn't enjoy the bond so much back then.

The shared experience of a common place takes all sorts of shapes, from a war endured together to a prison cell – the more intense the experience, the more enduring the identity. To be 'Kiwi' together is taken for granted at home. But when you're on the other side of the world, and you haven't been home for years, the like-no-other identity of being Kiwi can create overwhelming feeling. And even when we wear that identity lightly, even carelessly, back home, it can still surprise us with its power when the nation's yacht wins a race against an arrogant opponent, or an unlikely athlete wins an unexpected medal and shares the victory so we all feel involved.

Strong and well-established cultures that have long ago formed their like-no-other identity often resent younger, less certain cultures finding their own. 'Come and be like us,' they coo, which is another form of the old biblical problem of idolatry whereby you try to make the rest of the world in your own image. In the common search for what it is to be human, respect for difference is everything.

A hallmark of the divine Spirit is its capacity to uncover and treasure difference, even as it allows the diversity to co-exist.

So, for all its ambiguity, being Kiwi still counts. We can abuse the power of that like-no-other identity by using it as a jingoistic slogan to march us off to wars we shouldn't be fighting, or to suggest that it's more patriotic to play rugby than tennis, or to drink more beer of a particular brand, its German name notwithstanding. But the ease with which we abuse Kiwi identity only underlines the need to harness its power for good. As an adjective, it's at least as important to employ it before nouns like spirituality, as it is before politics or sport or agriculture.

Of course our spirituality in Aotearoa New Zealand is like some other kinds, and ultimately, because we are talking about something universal and eternal, it is like all other kinds. But you can't leapfrog your way into global identity without starting locally, discovering the value of where and who you are.

Of course these different levels of identity interlock together, one inside the other, like Russian babushka dolls. The outside shell impresses but the excitement comes from discovering the same impression inside, on a smaller but no less powerful scale.

We find it easier to deal with our identity in the larger sizes that fit everyone everywhere. But such outer garments are better worn with something more carefully tailored underneath to suit the shape of our particular bodies and souls. Our like-no-other Kiwi identity is an essential part of what we need to wear if we're to join the universal spiritual quest.

That essential Kiwi identity is itself made up of a whole series of related though no less vital identities; Maori, Pakeha, male and female, urban and rural, gay and straight – the list goes on. Our collective Kiwiness is a construct that evolves as the chemistry of these ingredients keeps shifting. The centre of this construct is less macho than it was a decade ago, the force of the Maori voice in the partnership is stronger, images of urban life now compete with farm and bush. Fred Dagg's caricatures of being Kiwi now look quaint and out of touch. The identity moves more quickly and it's harder to find ways whereby everyone can laugh at it together. Home-grown humour, always a precarious pursuit, is now the hardest job in town. The highest ratings go to yesterday's comedy. What makes us laugh about ourselves today is almost too painful to say out loud.

One reason is that local identities are always built around some sort of release. Dunedin-based Old Testament scholar Maurice Andrew shows that in his book, *Responding in Community*, where he describes the powerful identity of the Jews as bound up with their liberation from slavery in Egypt. The identity we all need for our spiritual journey involves us in finding our particular liberation.

What might that be for Pakeha people? Coming to terms with our ambiguous partnership with Maori and making good the abuses of the treaty covenant? Redressing the history of sectarian division and moralistic theology that our churches have produced? Acknowledging the shameful treatment of minority groups, both ethnic and ideological? Commitment to a new partnership that will make our institutions equitable and safe for women and men? Holding on to the hard-won dream of nuclear-free and easy, clean and green islands? Opening a dialogue of mutual respect between the living faith traditions represented here but until now muted by the voice of noisy, demonising Christians?

To be clear about which liberation struggle we need to engage in, and inevitably it will be a campaign on several fronts, is a prerequisite for discovering our Pakeha identity. And if that identity seems to be anaemic now, it could be that we haven't yet engaged fully or clearly enough with the forces that shape life and death in Aotearoa New Zealand.

Spirituality in general. Kiwi spirituality. There is all the difference in the world. Until we discover what Kiwi spirituality is, we'll go on discounting its power in favour of someone else's, easily borrowed. And it's not until we know it for ourselves as a Pakeha people that we can enjoy the playfulness that is the enduring hallmark of the Spirit moving, enabling us not to take ourselves and our struggles too earnestly.

>—◦—<

David Lange best summarised the cynicism about the whole business of being Maori or Pakeha in his first-hand account of a heart bypass operation in Green Lane Hospital. Filling in the admission form, he declared himself to be a Methodist on the grounds that it would protect him from being bothered by chaplains. Methodists are too busy these days with biculturalism, he declared, to be bothered about caring for people. That's a familiar line of argument aimed at all sorts of Pakeha groups, especially those with religious and spiritual interests, who seem preoccupied with their cultural identity at the expense of being human.

By Pakeha I mean the people other than Maori and Polynesian who belong here and nowhere else and whose contemporary culture lives here and nowhere else. It's a definition that Hamish Keith first coined and it still provides a good starting point for a definition mired in angry dispute. Pakeha may well be hyphenated people to recognise the part of them that lives somewhere else – such as Pakeha Scots or Chinese; there are even some Maori people who claim this hyphenated status. But hyphens are built into the business of being Pakeha. It is, after all, a relational word. It doesn't pretend to be complete and definitive by itself.

The unease about pursuing cultural identity too zealously points up a deeper spiritual unease and lack of confidence. The range of words and images that the Kiwi Spirit relies on for expression is pretty thin. When it comes to recognising God everywhere and forever, we are well equipped. There are lots of words and images and hymns to burn that praise a universal and eternal God who has been our help in ages past and will be in years to come; a God who holds the whole world in his hands; a God out there and up there, beyond and above the bright blue sky.

But when it comes to images of the God who is here and now, local, immediate and close up, then our repertoire is much more limited. What's more, for Pakeha New Zealanders, much of our repertoire is borrowed from somewhere else and some earlier time. We feel safer with words and sounds that have a little distance and formality, authorised by someone from somewhere else more important, preferably overseas. For most Christian traditions, the majority of the words and images come from Britain and Ireland and, more recently, from California; soon, they will come from Australia too.

Internally, we have made progress. There are authentically home-grown hymns and prayers and styles of religious life and some bold experiments in church government to respect the bicultural and multicultural structures of our nation. But there is no Pakeha equivalent to the Ringatu or Ratana movements. The nearest we had to an indigenous church structure was the ill-fated Plan for Union movement in the 1970s.

At the tail end of the twentieth century, the overwhelming impression remains of anything religious or spiritual being an additional extra to Pakeha culture, something we could do without as genuine Kiwis. Faced with this persistent sense of being irrelevant or marginal in the ebb and flow of Pakeha culture, religious interests withdraw from society and create independent, separate, self-defined communities. It's a pattern seen not only in newer groups like the Pentecostals and Eastern religions but also within mainstream denominations as their music and liturgy fails to make cultural connections with anyone under forty.

So what's needed? Neil Darragh is adamant that a radical ground-clearing operation is needed: 'what we need to do then from time to time is somehow to turn off the important and powerful theologies emanating from the older centres of Christianity. These theologies have their own legitimate agenda. But these agendas may be quite different, even alienating and destructive, from those required in a relatively new community just beginning to develop its own identity.'

For a realistic Roman Catholic to write like that is extraordinary, given the highly centralised form of that church, but his words underline the urgency of finding space for New Zealand pilgrims to pursue their faith journeys without constant reference to Rome or Canterbury or California. Expressions of the Kiwi Spirit shouldn't have to be checked with a head office anywhere. We don't need to dip into any font of superior spiritual wisdom to authenticate our religious experience.

We Pakeha have a bare century and a half of experience in this land, not much time to find the new words to describe spiritual experience. It's still easier to borrow from somewhere else and we used to borrow without stopping to think. But the old easy generalisations about all being New Zealand mates together in Maoriland have fallen apart. Now we tread carefully, for we tread not only on someone's dreams, as the Bremworth carpet ads used to say (with apologies to W.B. Yeats), but also on someone else's identity and perhaps their sovereignty as well. So we choose our words more carefully now. No wonder silence is becoming fashionable again in worship, or we look back with longing to the romantic simplicity of Celtic worship or Gregorian chant.

It's a hard time to be a Kiwi, let alone a Pakeha, and to find a way of saying what that means without appearing self-conscious and precious and stammering over the right words. But it's also the best time of all to be trying to find our tongues. Because we have the chance to discover what is distinctive about our heritage without it having to absorb and muddle other people's. There's an emerging respect for different cultural pathways (tikanga). No one pathway has to pretend to be complete and all embracing. Our incompleteness without each other is very clear.

James Belich's book *Making Peoples* demonstrates that vividly. You end it with an overwhelming sense that Pakeha people who can acknowledge their cultural interdependence with Maori can enjoy a sense of belonging here, far longer and richer than anything a Eurocentric focus can afford. Anne Salmond's book *Between Worlds* sharpens that sense of an intertwining spirituality. We are shaped by the very names we give each other – Maori and Pakeha – and the words make sense only as relational terms; as markers on a journey, in the Pakeha case, between being goblins with eyes in the back of our heads (as our forebears were seen) to becoming tangata tiriti – treaty people with a rightful place to stand. In the case of Maori, the journey is from New Zealander or native to noble but vanishing savage to tangata whenua today reclaiming (in every sense) the high ground, if you are Ngai Tahu, or the lakeshore if you are Tuhoe at Waikaremoana.

The biblical image of the tiny mustard seed applies here. However small, it grows amazingly on its own and takes its own distinctive shape and form, nurtured by a seemingly divine energy. A culture evolves in the same way, to contain all that is most precious, most distinctive, most visibly our own, all that gives us a collective voice and face unlike any other in the world.

So is there a song that Pakeha people can sing? A song of their own and not a kind loan from their Maori partners? Are there words and music written yet for the Kiwi blues? Our slowly emerging spirituality is best expressed in music because so much of it can't be said in words alone.

So how do we sing the blues in Aotearoa today? To answer that question you need to start with a story, just as the blues form itself began – out of a Black people's story that began somewhere between a slave ship from Africa and a cotton plantation in Mississippi.

So what stories will allow us to sing the blues in Aotearoa? There are plenty to choose from. The first one comes from Psalm 137 where the people of Israel are seated on the ground, by one of the canals that criss-crossed the plain between the Euphrates and the Tigris. They sit in the traditional posture of mourning, because they have been taken from their homeland into slavery in Babylon, and they are finding that unbearable. To make it worse, their captors ask them to sing, which is a cruel thing to ask of Jews, because all their songs are sacred, and to sing them on the foreign soil of an enemy is sacrilegious. So they hang up their harps in the willow branches along the riverbank as a musical act of defiance.

I don't think Te Maiharoa, Canterbury's greatest Maori prophet and peacemaker, would have felt like singing the blues when he wrote his petition to parliament back in 1881, demanding restoration of promised land. He saw that the Kemp settlement on the sale of Maori land had already been betrayed, and he was urged by many to resort to violence, yet he struggled to preserve the rule of law, even as he saw his people doomed to dispossession and exile. Te Maiharoa died as an old man at Korotuaheka at the mouth of the Waitaki River, oblivious to final ignominy of being refused permission by the Commissioner of Police to choose his burial place. His people didn't feel like singing the Aotearoa blues.

How can dispossessed people sing their song in a strange land? How can they make music when they have been betrayed? Instead of singing, the Jewish people go on, later in Psalm 137, to curse their captors. The psalm begins beautifully by the waters of Babylon but goes on to become an ugly cry of rage: 'Happy are those who take your children and smash them against a rock'.

This is the most violent verse in the Old Testament. Modern churches leave it out. Choirs don't try to sing it. Even in plainsong it's still frightening. But it's there in the Bible to remind us of the depth of righteous anger and alienation that dispossessed people do feel. When people wonder why the Treaty of Waitangi evokes such passionate protest, I read Psalm 137 and conclude that we get off lightly.

But the real surprise is not at the depth of cursing. It's the miracle of songs that go on being sung despite the dispossession and the pain.

In fact the Jews did go on singing through their exile; this psalm was written down much later. And Te Maiharoa's people went on singing. The petition to parliament lodged in 1881 has a much greater chance of being taken seriously now, given the recent rulings of the Waitangi Tribunal. Somehow, out of all that anger and betrayal, dispossessed people manage to keep singing, holding on to their hope of a heavenly city, their version of Jerusalem, by the waters of Babylon or the Waitaki.

When music is forged in suffering, it's called the blues. Not simply because it's often sad but, more importantly, because it's connected with the heart and built on the bedrock of the grief and sadness that go with being human. It's music that doesn't pretend that things are better than they really are, doesn't ignore past history or present pain. It's music that confronts the worst we have done and are doing to each other, and says that we can keep singing anyway, because there is still a hope of a better way.

That hope takes many forms. We dare not say that your hope should be mine. But we can trust that my inspiration might encourage yours. Three thousand years later, the psalmist's love for Jerusalem still lifts our spirits, and Te Maiharoa's brave letter can make us work harder to resolve old wrongs.

The hope might be for the right to return home, as it was for the psalmist, or the chance to 'build houses and inhabit them, to plant vineyards and eat their fruit', as it was for the prophet Isaiah, or the right to reclaim the land that was promised by the Crown, as it was for the prophet Te Maiharoa.

That's the kind of hope that lets us sing the Aotearoa blues. Concrete, practical hope for Maori and Pakeha, just as practical as the vision of Te Maiharoa, or Isaiah, or the exiles who wept by the waters of Babylon.

We can't afford to wait for those seemingly impossible visions to come to pass before we sing. We have to sing as we go, despite our cursing and our anger and our overwhelming sense of the unfairness and injustice of it all. It's out of that pain that the blues are born, the Aotearoa blues. If we could learn to sing them in English and in Maori, if we could share the verses of our song, then the music we made together would bring the justice and the healing we long to see.

Too hard? Could the right music really help? Do you remember the opening ceremony of the Atlanta Olympics, celebrating the Spirit of the South? And whose music did that multi-billion-dollar extravaganza rely on? The blues, of course, the songs of Black slaves. Imagine how they would have felt on those cotton plantations back at the time Te Maiharoa was writing his impossible petition, if they could have seen all that their music has achieved for their people, on their road to freedom. In 1995 their music inspired the world, a television audience of three and a half billion people.

Imagine what we could do, in this land, if we got the music right. We'd never have to write books wondering what we mean by a Kiwi spirituality.

CHAPTER 6

Please adjust the volume – hearing the Spirit

For townies, a bush walk after living in town requires more than a change of footwear. It takes some adjustment inside your head as well, so that you can hear the silence. Leave behind the noise of the car and the rest of your routine life; plunge into the quiet green. For the first minutes, it's as though there are no sounds beyond the rise of your own breath and the fall of your feet.

Then slowly, if you can resist the temptation to talk to yourself or turn on a transistor radio, the sounds of the bush start to seep through. Bird song, cicada screech, water running, leaves rustling and, hardest of all to hear, the energy of nature's life in foliage growing, dying, renewing.

We have to learn to listen to the silence of the bush. It's a basic discipline of Kiwi spirituality, but it's not something that Kiwi religions are good at teaching. Increasingly, our religious institutions are intent on making more noise rather than deciphering the silence. The marketing mania has engulfed religious institutions as it has every other part of our culture. Nothing is trusted any longer to speak for itself and even if it is true that 'by their fruits you shall know them', we can't afford to wait to find out.

So churches, temples and synagogues draw up marketing plans and promotional budgets like any other operation and look for ways to turn up the volume. How else do you get people to see and hear what you have to offer? If only we could make as much noise as the America's Cup or an All Black test series, if we only had a fraction of their media time, then religion of whatever kind would flourish in New Zealand overnight. Surely, a higher profile, more explicit, upfront, in-your-face brand of faith would do the trick.

Our history suggests otherwise. What works for selling soap powder or boat racing doesn't translate directly for things spiritual. Where preachers have shouted loudest and the message has been most explicit and direct, the negative reaction has been strongest. The history of Protestant piety in this country, writes Massey University historian Peter Lineham, has been one of great ambivalence. He traces a detailed picture through the nineteenth century of a strong distaste for noisy excesses and overstatement by churches, even when these came in the well-tested form of revivalism – the loudest and most explicit packaging of religious experience. The revival meetings on the early New Zealand circuit became comparatively subdued gatherings. 'The traditional indicators of religious experience – frenzy, vision and healing – were largely absent from colonial evangelism,' writes Lineham. He concludes that the institutional churches have failed to recreate vital forms of piety in this country, and in their struggle to be effective have become 'large and active clerical organisations with vociferous moral tones'.

The less effective our institutions are, the noisier they become. There is a devastating piece of social commentary, popular as an embroidered mantelpiece feature in Victorian times, that still applies: 'It thundereth so loud what you say/That it cannot be heard what you are'. Instead of being a measure of confidence and strength, a dominant, high-profile, loud and explicit presentation can speak of anxiety and confusion. Commercial businesses that sell frantically and promise the earth with once-only bargains soon arouse distrust among consumers. Media advertising that constantly inflates and dramatises soon builds up a customer resistance. The explicit TV commercials in the anti-drink-drive campaign seem quickly to create a viewer fatigue as we react self-protectively against such concentrated doses of blood and gore.

Such commercials are built on the same premise as the old-fashioned hellfire and brimstone sermon – the more explicit the portrayal, the stronger the effect. But the value of this approach seems very short-term, at least in the New Zealand context. What's more, it begs some unspoken lessons that our emerging Kiwi spirituality has to teach us – namely that there seems to be a preference built into Pakeha culture for a quiet, subtle style of communication. Modest, understated, self-effacing models win enduring respect, ahead of the noisy self-promoters.

Spiritual discipline of any sort has always valued that which is hidden and implicit. When it comes to discerning the Spirit, slow and careful watching and waiting are the hallmarks, making sure the elegance and self-importance of the observer don't get in the road.

In the Judaeo-Christian tradition, those whom God uses most powerfully are invariably spiritual stumblebums, slow to see and understand, reluctant to keep trying, comprehending in hindsight, if at all. Only a handful of biblical figures have visions of God and, when they do, their skin and clothing are burnt and bleached, for the intensity of divine encounter is too terrible for normal humans. Those who claim God's direct illumination are, more often than not, kept in psychiatric care. The human way to know God is through the relationships and covenants, the hints and glimpses that the created world provides. Incarnation is the formal word for this. In essence, the way we need to follow and the truth we need to know are ours for the asking, where and as we are. We don't have to leave home to find the Kiwi Spirit, even if we're slow to see it. That's par for the course.

Every religious tradition is caught in the tension between saying too much and too little about God. Pakeha religion, despite its short history, has definitely erred on the side of saying too much, too soon, about too many things. The credibility test for establishing an enduring Kiwi spirituality will lie in our discipline to live with the incomplete and the unfinished, to value silence and waiting, to resist grabbing for attention and visibility we can't sustain.

For the immediate future, Kiwi spirituality is likely to require a low-key style, for nothing discourages Pakeha people more that the embarrassment caused by those who speak too loudly and publicly about the really important things. To shout about God is like talking to strangers about how you make love. The Kiwi face of the Spirit is revealed in bits and pieces, slowly, in fragments over time, here, there and everywhere. Those who claim too loudly to have seen too much, too soon, will not be believed.

Chapter 7

Urban spirituality
– learning to love the city

It's a whole lot easier to talk about Kiwi spirituality with tui and bellbirds trilling in the bush, and green hills to look out on and lift our eyes towards. It's much harder in a city, surrounded by concrete and pollution, with a fair chance of getting mugged on the way home. On the face of it, an urban spirituality is more likely to be about pessimism and despair.

Take the campaign to stop psychiatric services from moving out of rural Tokanui into the middle of Hamilton. Patients past and present organised a petition to stop the move. 'Tokanui is a beautiful place with its trees and lawns,' they told television news. 'There's nothing at Waikato Hospital for our healing. Nothing. Just city. No nature there, only concrete jungle.'

Remember the movie *Once Were Warriors* – as bleak a vision of our urban landscape as we've ever seen on the big screen. At one point the central family, torn apart by the violence and despair they inhale from the streets of South Auckland, almost manage to escape from the city for a day. The countryside is idyllic, Maoritanga is still intact out there, but they're drawn back to the trashy parking lot of the pub, and their lives start to disintegrate again. There is redemption, finally, for some, but it comes in spite of the city and only with the support of elders from a rural marae.

The only really hopeful urban symbol of faith I can recall in New Zealand movies comes in Vincent Ward's *The Navigator*, where the young boy manages to plant a cross on the spire of St Patrick's Cathedral in Auckland. But he has to come from the thirteenth century in England to do that and, as if by way of a warning, he falls back into that era again.

These are examples from the so-called secular world. Have our religious institutions got a better record in finding urban spirituality? The national programme for Spiritual Growth Ministries lists several opportunities for directed retreats, using the language of silence and contemplation. Not surprisingly, many are offered in rural settings. There's one, however, in Glenfield called a Street Retreat for those 'interested in discovering God's presence in the inner city'. But where exactly? 'Among the poor, in the harshness and power of social structures that hurt and oppress them.'

In the countryside, it seems that we expect to find God in beauty and solitude. In the city, look to the pain and the chaos, if you are to find God there at all. Why is that we start so hesitantly and negatively when we look for God in the city? (By 'we', I speak only as a middle-aged Pakeha male. My children are more positive, though they wouldn't ask the question in the same way.)

One reason is that we don't think we've been here long enough. 'The plains are nameless and the cities cry for meaning, the unproved heart still seeks a vein of speech,' wrote Charles Brasch half a century ago. His answer was to experience a century of solitude and to lie like a lover, not with the 'stunted township' but with the gaunt hills. They're from whence our help might come.

Allen Curnow, in the same era, wrote in the same vein, meditating on the great moa in the Canterbury Museum. He saw it as an 'interesting failure to adapt' and wondered whether 'Not I, [but] some child, born in a marvellous year/ Will learn the trick of standing upright here.' Curnow's children have grown up now and the marvellous year has not arrived when we can stand tall and easy in our landscape, urban or rural, as Pakeha. Where can we celebrate a Kiwi spirituality? What is it that keeps us down and holds us back?

Our inherited Protestant piety has a lot to answer for. This invariably worked from the inside outwards. You started very personally and privately with a heart and soul, black or white, hot or cold. Get that right with God and everything else followed, whether you were in darkest Africa or the remote colony of New Zealand. The idea of a God who was equally interested in working from the outside inwards, to use Dietrich Bonhoeffer's phrase, who might be speaking to us through culture or creation itself, a God who might be present ahead of us, in the landscape, let alone the cityscape – well, that was more than our inherited piety could imagine.

Against that background, it's not surprising that an urban spirituality has been so slow to develop here. Any sort of spirituality that trusts God working from the outside in has been stunted, whether through culture or environment or economy.

There's also a deeper problem in Western theology that predates Victorian piety. It's a distrust of the physical, certainly of the body, as a channel or domain of grace. Never mind the classic understanding of incarnation that anchors divinity in the dust and sweat of humanity and history. We still fondly believe that spiritual things are above material, that spirit outranks matter every time and that blood and sweat and skin are a slightly improper domain for the divine.

This is still a very popular heresy, cultivated by the Steven Spielberg school of cinema, which holds that any close encounter with mystery has to be of a third or fourth kind, but never down-to-earth for long. Science fiction movies delight in this anti-matter ideology, as do television advertisements where truth, meaning and dollar value are recognised by the light and warmth that is radiated by the lounge suite or the soup packet.

All of this makes it hard to believe that technology, around which urban life is framed, could ever be a vehicle of God's presence and truth. Myron Bloy, Episcopal Chaplain at the Massachusetts Institute of Technology, wrote a book that challenged this ethereal, other-worldly nonsense. During a woodcutting trip, he was inspired by a young engineering student's mastery of a chainsaw, marvelling at the youth's easy, confident skill in using this dangerous tool to control and create a good result. *The Gracefulness of Technology* is the title of Bloy's book – a bold celebration of the state of grace that urban technology just might contain.

A final word about the obstacles that stop the city speaking about the spirit must concern the fragmentation and dislocation of urban community. It's not that community isn't there; it's just so disparate and broken up into scattered bits and pieces, the alienation is so intense, the divide between rich and poor so extreme, that all our usual language of spirituality breaks down. Maybe God does meet us in tension, noise and chaos, but we've lost the words, if we ever had them, to describe the encounter.

But through all the obstacles to an emerging urban spirituality, the excitement of the city still seeps through and influences our piety, in spite of ourselves. By excitement, I mean what the dictionary says when you look up the word: 'to set in motion, to rouse and stir up, to stimulate into activity'. How does God set us in motion through the urban environment? What are the signs of that engagement?

Many of us are trained to respect those signs in the food banks and soup kitchens, the coalitions for justice in housing and health and all the traditional models of social service that try to respond to the poor and the alienated. More elusive is the excitement prompted by the freedom that the city promises, especially to those of us brought up in rural New Zealand. Our cities are full of rural refugees, escaping not only from the lack of job and educational opportunity, but also from the isolation, the unrelenting orthodoxy, the suffocating pressure of family and tight community that country life so often creates. The open spaces are rural in a geographical sense, but to find the open spaces of the mind and heart and imagination, where the boundaries of possibility are pushed back, give me a crowded city street any day.

It's there we taste the diversity that we know life contains because we hear about it overseas, and long to see and sample it at home. Slowly, our cities are beginning to reveal that diversity in shops which let you buy what you like, theatres and mass media which let you see and hear what you like, restaurants which let you eat what you like, colour combinations and fashion codes which let you wear what you like. There's no way this freedom to choose can be reined in. An urban spirituality has to respect that variety is here to stay and become open-ended, multi-faceted, pluralistic, ecumenical. Any dogmatic or authoritarian attempt to impose a return to a one-way, single-track, more uniform spirituality is doomed to separate us from the city.

City life is a marvellous balancing act between confusion and control. It survives and grows through a delicate chemistry conjured up by engineers and artists, politicians and computer programmers. Everything looks as though it's built to last forever – until the drains block, the traffic jams, the toilets won't flush and the lights go out. Auckland's water and power crises reminded us of that. A city of glass-towered self-sufficiency had to go begging for a drink and a shower and a candle in the darkness.

Live in a city for any length of time and you can't help getting caught up in that tension between sublime confidence and complete chaos. Dozens of movies have exploited the anxiety of living in this tension. On the one hand, anything goes and everything is possible. You can say and do what you like. Nobody cares. On the other, there are limits and controls everywhere. Everybody's watching. It's a miracle the place survives. And it does so only through human imagination and ingenuity. It's not old nature's magic or some mysterious force that's bigger than all of us. It's people wheeling, dealing and building community that keeps the city alive. It's an activity that begs to be valued theologically, if only we could find the words.

In the natural world, the processes that keep creation turning are all well hidden, camouflaged behind the cycle of seasons and the subtle balance of plant and animal ecosystems. We wait till things go wrong before we understand what was needed to keep everything right. In the city we build our own creation. You can see the scaffolding and the wires. If it doesn't work, we tear it down, as we've done in every New Zealand city except Dunedin. We understand it because we and our forebears put it there. The interplay of forces that will keep it there is in our hands. We are responsible, and there's no one else, not even God, to blame.

All of that gives us the freedom to get on with the task of becoming human. It creates the climate for a spirituality centred on each other's limitless potential and adaptability rather than on superstition about hidden powers and unseen forces. What matters is how well we connect and communicate. A spirituality of engagement, not withdrawal, is what the city offers, if we have eyes to see.

How then might we begin to shape such a spirituality that respects the hallmarks of the city – its precarious freedom, its endless diversity, its often uncomfortable tension between severe limits and unrestricted licence? These are the hallmarks that shape the lives of city people. A faith that doesn't respect these features will end up as an escape hatch, which is what the church has so often provided for urban dwellers.

Let's start with the constraints we have to recognise if we're to avoid a Pollyanna piety. Gail Ramshaw's book *Searching for Language* is very helpful at this point. She talks about the need to see human limitation as a positive fact in faith and worship. Our spiritual quest is all about finding our place as women and men within a community and a creation that is in right relationship with God. The Jewish people call that condition 'shalom'. Joan Puls describes it with the image of the seagull, hovering high in the wind, perfectly in tune with the elements, flying as it was meant to, effortlessly. Images like the seagull, conditions like shalom, don't complain about the limitations of being human, finite, mortal. They celebrate such boundaries.

Unfortunately, in the Western Christian tradition, this fact of limitation has been narrowed down to language about human frailty. It's invariably called sin and we're repeatedly asked to feel bad about it and seek forgiveness for it. But you could equally well, in biblical terms, describe human limitation using images of justice and injustice, or disease and wholeness, or death and life, or chaos and meaning. What is desperately needed is a new flexibility to adapt our forms of spirituality so that they resonate with the images that best fit people's context and experience.

So which of these descriptions of human limitation best fits urban life? The answer will differ perhaps from city to city. Perhaps it is the tension between chaos and meaning that dominates. Consider, for example, the seemingly endless power of the city to make everything and everyone relative to and conditional on something else, the ease with which the city can isolate and overwhelm us, to leave us feeling utterly alone in the midst of the crowd, the savagery with which the city's structures can make us rich and popular one minute, destitute and forgotten the next.

Urban life is the venue for the most soul-destroying experience, and the most stimulating and satisfying search for understanding. Even more than for jobs and money, we come to the city for recreation and education, for artistic and intellectual challenge. And people who stand up in the city to offer roadmaps out of personal and spiritual chaos into meaning and sanity draw the most extraordinary response. Look at the crowds that a Lloyd Geering or a John

Spong can attract, to say nothing about less orthodox gurus of new age and liberation.

New Zealand has one of the highest rates of teenage suicide in the developed world. One of the reasons, we're told, is the loss of meaning that young people experience in our brave, new, high-tech, jobless society, which gives us the freedom to do anything, yet be nothing. A spirituality that speaks credibly about human limitation and the meaning and purpose we derive from finding a place to stand in the city, that would be a timely gift indeed.

Through our religious traditions we inherit a treasure chest of resources from our past concerning spiritual discipline, psychological health, literary and visual arts, models of community, intergenerational learning, rituals of healing, affirmation and empowerment, words and music for therapy, meditation and inspiration. But our ability to open and share that treasure chest with a secular society bored by institutional religion is constantly frustrated by those who insist that the treasures are for members only. Name the name first, confess your sin, then meaning can follow. The effect of such an approach is to ensure that the riches of our religious heritage are shared with fewer and fewer people, and the wall between so-called secular and sacred grows higher by the day.

A spirituality of engagement isn't preoccupied with trying to protect and copyright religious meaning and it has no patience with dualistic divisions between secular and sacred. The classical language of prayer, so concerned with preparation and purification, withdrawing and ascending, perfecting and improving, doesn't help much here. Engagement implies a coming ready or not theology, a willingness to start as and where we are with what we've got.

So what action is this spirituality of engagement leading us toward? I think it's to do with befriending the city, being present on the streets, in the pubs and clubs and cinemas, helping to reclaim the night and the dark corners of the city by being there ourselves, and finding others to come with us.

Much of that we might be doing already for work, or fun, because we get paid to, or because we enjoy it, but it goes beyond this. It involves the risk of expecting to find God through that urban engagement, in the midst of the noise and the smoke and the hustle and the wheeling and dealing, in the crowds and the compromises, the pressure and stress, in the words on the concrete walls and the boarding house halls.

F.D. Maurice put it like this: 'Must I utterly renounce all things about me that I may be absorbed into God, or is there any way in which I can devote them and myself to God, and only know God the better by fitting my place among them?' Maurice answers our question about an urban spirituality. To find God we fit into the city, listening for the one who is 'nearer than breathing, closer than hands or feet', the one we can't see for looking. The one who is to be found in the most ordinary and everyday.

George McLeod of the Iona Community quotes a story that shows just how close and how ordinary this God of the city is. It concerns a go-getter businessman who had gone to a group of Zen Buddhist monks for enlightenment, which wasn't coming – and certainly not quickly enough.

'What is the ultimate word of truth anyway?' he demanded.

'Yes,' said the monk.

'And why haven't you been instructing me about reality?' he demanded.'

'When you brought me tea, did I not drink it? When you served me food, did I not eat it?' replied the monk.

'I've been here for a week and I still can't find your school,' said the exasperated executive.

'It's this table and this chair,' replied the monk. 'This fireplace and this window.'

'Well then, what is this religious life?' was the final question.

And the monk replied, 'In the early morning, how do you do. In the evening, good night.'

If we really could bring ourselves to believe that God's presence was that close, then the practice of our spirituality would be very different. It would take on the colours and cultures of our surroundings much more rapidly and easily than it does.

I'm fascinated by the very different speeds at which we move on these issues of making theology and worship indigenous. Pacific Island communities in New Zealand, despite their strong history of Victorian evangelical piety, still manage, in their worship, to ensure the inclusion of the distinctive rhythms and idioms of their island cultures, while adapting to meet the new demands of being Kiwi. So there are PIC (Pacific Island Church) netballers and rap music groups and, who knows, a PIC league team in the Winfield Cup in years to come.

The pace of Pakeha cultural adaptation is glacial by comparison. We hug our old and bygone hymns, keep importing preachers and their language from the United States and England, seemingly oblivious to the distancing effect this has on the God who waits to meet us in our own cities, speaking our own languages and singing our own melodies.

Not that there is any neutral place to stand as we attempt this adaptation of the spiritualities we inherit. To become too purist about the need to start afresh, free from all the old captivities and compromises, can be both precious and paralysing. We can transform what we've got, as well as, and alongside, letting some of it go. A spirituality of engagement can lead us down both paths and we can share stories from both journeys. Unhappily, the two sets of travellers, those who want to hold on to the past and those who let it go, are not good at talking to each other.

In the movie *L.A. Story*, Steve Martin has long conversations with the traffic signs on the freeway. He sees the words on these signs rearrange themselves into helpful advice, so he stops and has a chat. So in tune is he with his urban environment that even the highway technology responds to his need. 'Who is this man that even wind and sea obey him?' the disciples ask each other after Jesus calms the storm on the Sea of Galilee. Well, Steve Martin doesn't quite reach that stage but he's in tune with one of the most difficult cities in the world. He loves the place. He has enormous expectations that it will be good to him. He understands Los Angeles because he has spent a lifetime listening to it. He believes wholeheartedly in its potential, refuses to be frightened by it and revels in its freedom and variety. In the midst of chaos, Steve finds meaning enough, for the time being.

Surprise, surprise, he never mentions an urban spirituality of engagement during the whole movie. But if I were to ask him what it means, he'd understand immediately.

Chapter 8

The myth of safe harbours – facing the storm

Places for spiritual gathering are the safest places to be, and the most dangerous. Cathedrals, churches, synagogues, temples and whare karakia have always acted as sanctuaries from the threats of the world outside. In the Middle Ages, churches provided refuge for victims of injustice from tyrant kings who were afraid of nothing except the spiritual authority of the church – and not even that at times. So prisoners on the run and political agitators would hide under spiritual protection. Heretics had to be more careful.

Spiritual places today, even in secular New Zealand, continue this role of refuge and safe haven for people and communities battered by the storms of everyday life and death. For example, to many sick and troubled and dying people in Christchurch, the cathedral in the Square plays that role of safe harbour, not only through the care they receive from the community of faith that worships there, but also from the comfort and strength people draw from the light and space of the cathedral – the architecture, the sense of history, of being surrounded by other sailors who have gone before us, the power of the music and the liturgy, and the freedom that comes from being welcome at any time, whoever you are.

The community, too, needs the cathedral. When Christchurch loses a hero like Rob Hall or Charles Upham, or when people are faced with the horror of the Tiananmen Square massacre, or the sadness of losing the city's big red public buses, then the cathedral is used as a safe place to do the crying and remembering.

And all of that is well and good, until religious and spiritual values become no more than safety nets, setting up spiritual places like the cathedral as sanctuaries to run to, with something to say to those who come in, but not much to say when you go out, especially if there's a storm blowing outside.

Much of my life is spent inside the Gothic cathedral where I work. It gives every appearance of being a solid citadel of faith; its music and liturgy express a secure heritage and a confident spirituality. But to remind me of the cathedral's unfinished task, I keep pinned to my office wall a sign that reads: 'Trailers for sale or rent, rooms to let – 50 cents'. The words come from that well-known country and western song, *King of the Road*, which is all about life on the highway, as transient, uncomfortable and dangerous as any journey could be, still travelling, still a long way from home.

Because the trouble with safe harbours is that they so easily become landlocked. Their entrances silt over, bars of sand form across their mouths and their promise of safety disappears. If you're a Greymouth fishing boat coming home and a storm gets up, the safe thing to do is stay out at sea, way out, and steam down to Jacksons Bay. A line of memorial plaques on the Greymouth breakwater testify to those who dreamt of home as safe harbour, but never made it over the port's treacherous river bar.

The greatest disillusion about a safe harbour I ever experienced was in Dunedin, where I learnt to love and trust the Otago Harbour, sailing and fishing and exploring its every corner. It became, for me, the ultimate safe place, temperamental, of course, but reliable and beautiful in every way. I produced a programme for National Radio about it, with lyrical meditations about the assurance of the sweep of the hills down to the water, the confidence of its long 20-kilometre reach up to the city, the grace of its little islands and bays, and the welcome of the settlement that guarded the mouth to the harbour, a village whose Maori name means 'Gateway to the Sea'.

And then, one weekend in 1990, all that changed. Aramoana, as the village was called, became the scene of New Zealand's worst massacre, a prelude to Port Arthur, and for me and thousands of others, my safe harbour was no longer safe. I had trusted too much in my sanctuary. I had used it as a place to come into and stay in. I had not used its strength for going out and living in the storms.

All of this is very hard to speak or sing about. Most of our songs about the sea tell of coming home and of the joy of safe harbours. It's much easier to write music for 'Home is the sailor, home from the sea' than about heading out to the depths of the unknown. But it is precisely out there, in those depths, that we find the most reliable and enduring images of spiritual life.

Promises of safe harbour are two a penny: from life insurance companies, private medical packages, wholewheat breakfast foods, special offers from banks and a hundred weekend seminars that guarantee wholeness, macrobiotic vibrations and spiritual wellbeing in three days. But there aren't so many offers for a faith that will get you through the storms.

When I look back on my Otago Harbour experiences, I realise that the best image of faith was not the safety of sailing inside, but the day when we were nearly lost outside the entrance.

We were trolling just across the harbour mouth and a line became entangled in the propeller. A southerly squall got up out of nowhere and within minutes we were drifting well out from the cliffs around the entrance, in ever higher waves that made the land behind us harder and harder to see. And the nearest land ahead was the coast of Chile.

What saved us was the teamwork of our crew, our ability to use the resources we had inside the boat, the knowledge of what we could and couldn't do (mostly what we couldn't), and the trust we had in each other. I learnt more about faith from that experience than from a thousand reassurances inside safe harbours where I was never tested beyond my limits, never challenged, never forced to discover my interdependence with others.

The same harbour and the endless stretch of the ocean outside its mouth has inspired Dunedin hymn writer Colin Gibson to find these words:

> When the coast is left and we journey on
> to the rim of the sky and the sea,
> be the sailor's friend, be the dolphin Christ.
> lead us on to eternity.
>
> When the clouds are low and the wind is strong,
> when tomorrow's storm draws near,
> be the spirit bird hovering overhead
> who will take away our fear.

The hymn is a powerful one to sing together. It taps into the risk and fear that empty, overwhelming ocean conjures up for many New Zealanders. The request for God's guidance and presence in this encircling sea beyond our control is not a plea for a secure return to a safe harbour. Gibson's words simply ask for company on a journey that we know will be hazardous and uncertain.

A friend came to me recently to talk about the emptiness of his life after losing a loved one. Still grieving, he talked about the way his loss had shattered his old certainties. He used to have a clear-cut faith, hold very forthright opinions. Now he wasn't so sure any more. Life had become infinitely more complicated and more mysterious. He worried that all that was a sign of spiritual decay. I tried to suggest that it might be a sign of spiritual growth.

Living in the storms outside the harbour is not easy, never certain, but it is the place we're meant to be and it is the place where faith is lost and found, the only place where any sort of enduring faith is to be discovered.

If visits to spiritual places like cathedrals and churches help us to live out there in the storm of life, in the midst of relationships that won't go right, and kids who won't behave and parents who won't listen, and sickness and tragedy that continue to strike the wrong people at the wrong time (people like us who don't deserve it) – if we get that help from spiritual places, well and good.

If we don't, then let's close the doors. Because we don't need the false promise of any more safe harbours, because somewhere, sometime, there's always a town called Aramoana across the entrance.

Out in the storm is the place to be, because that's where God is to be found. The psalmist tells us that. God's arms undergird all the storms across all the seas. God's energy enlivens all the living things both small and great in the sea and, just for fun, God throws in a couple of leviathans to fool around in the waves with a slow flick of their giant tails, just as they do off the coast of Kaikoura.

One contemporary blessing invokes the wildness and the warmth of God. It could equally well invoke the cold and the wet of God, the drenching spray, the bite of the salt and the lash of the sea wind, the untamed and inexplicable energy of the storm that is our life, outside the safety of the harbour. Out there, in all of that, God waits to meet us. In daring to believe that, in hoping and trusting that something so impossible could be true, we find our real safety.

Katherine Mansfield, whose tragically short life was all too often lived out in the storm, perhaps understood this paradox. One of her favourite quotations, inscribed on the stone slab that marks her grave in France, was Hotspur's words from *Henry IV, Part I*: 'But I tell you, my lord fool, out of this nettle, danger, we pluck this flower, safety'.

CHAPTER 9

Green thumbs and green souls
– the holy ground of gardens

More and more New Zealanders are living out their lives through their gardens. Increasingly, trees, flowers and lawns count for more than the jobs we have or used to have, the houses we live in, the cars we drive or the children we have reared. It's gardening that lights us up and connects us with the spiritual realm – the things of beauty and mystery, the processes of change and growth beyond our understanding, the chemistry of colour, form and scale.

Maybe that's why increasing numbers of people want to get married in the garden. If the law allowed it, they'd get buried there too. In our so-called secular society, gardens become our chapels and our shrines. They are, for many people, holy ground. And they provide the location for and the means to do some holy things, such as remembering and honouring our dead.

Have you noticed the increasing number of flowers left along the fencelines or against the telegraph poles of our highways where people have been killed in accidents? Most of these bouquets aren't professional products from the florist shop. They come from home gardens, grown with personal care and left with love. On the roadside at Raurimu, the latest scene of mass murder in New Zealand, flowers were left for weeks after the tragedy. Truck drivers, not usually thought of as flower people, stopped their huge vehicles at the site of the massacre to leave floral tributes. Passing motorists paid their respects. Strangers who wanted to share the weight of the grief and the tragedy could say it with flowers, their flowers, when their words couldn't be heard.

We use our gardens to remember, to honour, to mourn, to pour out our anger, to connect with our past, to claim our heritage, be that last week's tragedy, or a horror story fifty years old. I recently visited Stan Graham's grave on the West Coast, where the trauma of those killings is still experienced half a century on. Someone is still putting flowers on his plain concrete tomb, and on those of the two home guardsmen, shot down in this lone farmer's rampage.

Equally important, we use our gardens and their produce to look forward, to speak not only of what might have been, but also of what might still be. Through the energy and time and, of course, the money we give to our gardens, we're claiming the future and trying to shape it. We complain about the rise in the cost of movie tickets that buy our dreams in celluloid, but happily spend twice as much on a plant that we won't see in blossom for years to come, if we see it at all.

Our confidence in gardens as vehicles of dreams is boundless, and it grows by the day as we watch those gardening shows on television where a decade of back-wrenching work and a budget big enough for two world tours is reduced to five easy minutes of lawns and trees and flower beds filmed to look as though they've always been there.

One of these days, a TV producer is going to discover the Book of Revelation, which has a gardening story to beat them all. There you have a location in the time of a new heaven and a new earth, with the river of life running through it and a tree of life on either bank. Can you imagine how beautiful that tree would look? And all around there are gardens with fruit trees that are harvested constantly through the year. What would ENZA do with that? And the leaves of the plants in this garden provide healing balm for the nations of the world. There is nothing accursed in this garden, no disease, no wrecking winds and hailstorms. It is perfect.

It all sounds out of this world, doesn't it? Yet it's a vision that is closer to home than we know. It's the vision that shaped the early Pakeha settlement of this country, as James Belich's history of New Zealand, *Making Peoples*, shows. In what Belich calls the crusader literature used to lure our great-grandparents into making a dangerous sea voyage to the unknown, other side of the world, Edward Gibbon Wakefield and others promoted the image of New Zealand as Arcadia and Utopia – the perfect garden that used to be, and the perfect place that could be. Listen to these book titles published between 1850 and 1880: *The Wonderland of the Antipodes, An Earthly Paradise, The Eden of the World, The Land of Milk and Honey* and, perhaps less ambitious, *Brighter Britain. The Land of Promise.*

And the promise was delivered in well-publicised stories of gardens which grew exotic flowers that would never bloom in Birmingham, and vegetables you could only dream about in Brixton. Stories were sent home about 4-kilogram carrots growing in Christchurch and a 25-kilogram cabbage in Dunedin. Who could prove it? Who would want to eat it, anyway? When he arrived, Wakefield found the place to be a vegetable paradise and he saw the whole country through 'carrot-tinted spectacles'.

There is a more ambiguous side to these dreams at the bottom of our colonial gardens. These early crusaders were both ignorant and scornful about the native plants and fruits that were here, likening them to turpentine and wizened quince. They knew nothing about the skill of the Maori gardeners who were here before them, although they relied heavily on the produce of the tangata whenua. Slash and burn, rather than conserve and adapt, was usually the motto.

The dreams of Arcadia and Utopia drove the settlers not into romance but into the reality of technology and politics that moved at breakneck speed. Progress was everything – farms and gardens brought into production, bush cleared, roads cut and rails laid. There was nothing natural or organic or ecological or sustainable about any of this.

At the end of the twentieth century, we're finally beginning to see the settler myths that shaped our Pakeha beginnings here. The gardens we inherit speak volumes about the sort of people we have become and the dreams that drive us. We are more sober than our forebears about visions of controlling and owning the land and its produce on our terms. Issues of treaty and ecology and free trade and world markets become entangled in our dreams. Our gardens become parables of struggle and disappointment as much as promises of a new heaven and a new earth.

But the power of the garden to inspire and to speak of the Spirit remains: to move us, as good music can, into a wider, deeper realm of being and, in the process, grow a resilient spirituality. That power can give us the strength to acknowledge the mistakes we have made as a people, and show us new and better ways to be caretakers of the earth, partners in God's clean and green creation. To keep it clean and green is as much a spiritual as an economic and political discipline. Kiwis in future are going to need green souls as well as green thumbs.

Chapter 10

Three trees and a truck
– the divine in the ordinary

Between two trees, there lies a story true.' It's a song we used to sing on the school bus. Fifty years later I've found another true story between three beech trees on the roadside near Greymouth. They stand as a group, just clear of the bushline, relating easily to each other, separate yet interdependent, confident and beautiful, at home in the soil, blending with the other foliage around them. Somehow, each time, I feel better after seeing these trees. For me, they mark the beginning or the end of a journey.

Like the corny old song about the soldier and the pack of cards that he uses as a prayer book and a Bible, the three trees can serve as an image of the Trinity – the three-way conversation between creating, redeeming and giving of life that lies at the heart of the Christian understanding of God. But before that kind of conceptual thinking lies the discovery that ordinary, physical things can be the substance and the means of something holy and divine. I can trust God to meet me in three old trees.

Or old door knockers, for that matter. That claim comes from G.K. Chesterton, who saw such common objects as signs of God. And if door knockers don't do much for you, then remember this strange truth, he wrote, 'that things seemingly substantial are really spiritual, is even better proved from unpleasant than from pleasant things'. A piece of salmon, he argued, can be as poetic and splendid as a sunset.

Writing two centuries earlier, on the other side of the Atlantic, the New England Puritan preacher Jonathan Edwards spelt out the connection between the divine and ordinary physical things more soberly. God meets us, he wrote, 'in and through experience of an encounter with a definite, concrete, substantial being and not in and through the abstract, ethereal, incommunicable or untouchable'.

Nothing in my formal religious training had prepared me to see three beech trees as more than wood and leaves. Physical and spiritual realities were well fenced off from each other in my head, as they are in the heads of many Pakeha New Zealanders.

Mike Crowl, writing in the *Dunedin Star Midweek* and wondering why our newspapers devote space to sport rather than religion, said: 'this tells us a lot about ourselves as a nation; we're focused on the physical, the material, the tangible. We shy away from the aesthetic, the spiritual, the things that endure, or the things with a sense of the eternal about them.'

But I'm finding by the day that Mr Crowl was posing a false choice as the so-called physical things start to speak more loudly of mystery and possibility than the so-called spiritual things. A walk on the beach, a shared meal, a hand held tightly, a newly mown lawn, an old hat badge my great-grandfather wore have all, for me, taken on a spiritual meaning richer and deeper than many inherited symbols of faith.

There is a New Testament passage where Jesus tells some not very clever disciples that even the stones of the street cry out when people who ought to understand cannot see or hear. The passage haunts me because it is the story of my own journey in faith – a progress from believing that the best images of faith were borrowed and inherited, to finding that there are more telling images all around me, close to home.

But that seemingly obvious shift in location couldn't happen without the insight that the divine is to be found in ordinary, everyday things, here and now. An unholy alliance has been formed in our Pakeha religious experience between the otherworldly and the other side of the world – spirituality and geography fused to confuse us.

Rather than theologians it has been poets such as Richard Wilbur who have helped me untangle that confusion. In a poem entitled *Love calls us to the things of this world*, Wilbur writes of a man awakening to the sounds and smell of laundry being hung to dry in the sun:

> Outside the open window
> The morning air is awash
> with angels.

That way of seeing the washing, and the world, makes it infinitely easier to look for and expect to find a spirituality of this time and place, anchored in the ordinary things that happen, even in the trees you drive past on the road.

That's the encouraging part. The silly part is that I've never bothered to stop as I drive by and walk over to look at those three trees. I think I'm afraid that, up close, they may not prove to be as mysterious.

>—⊶•⊙•⊷—<

When I pass those three trees on my way to or from the West Coast, I'm usually driving my truck. It's a fairly ordinary truck as trucks go these days. Not even a four-wheel drive, which is almost compulsory if you want any street credibility in the Christchurch suburbs (for who knows when you might run into a snowstorm or a mudslide on your way to work). But it is a diesel, 2.7 litres no less, with a tuffdeck and a double cab, fog lights, backing mirrors and crash bars. No gun rack. No off-road tyres. But you can't have everything.

It's just a basic truck and that has huge advantages.

For one thing, it's easy to see when it's overloaded. Lift the cover, check the curve of the high slung springs and you can see right away if you're attempting too much. And so can everyone else. It is only the lightest of utility vehicles. Big loads have to be shared with others. My limits are easy to see.

Which is more than you can say for our Kiwi churches – vehicles that are constantly overloaded. We expect them to be full of nice people pleasing everyone and doing worthy things, growing by the week and getting everyone to agree on what to believe. I think it's time we saw the churches and all places of religious gathering as more like my truck: a vehicle for a journey, with room for all kinds of ordinary passengers, who are free to get off and on where they choose; a vehicle that breaks down, gets stuck, needs repairs and, when it's overloaded, needs to be lightened up, to share its load and to stop pretending it's the only truck on the road.

The other advantage about my truck is that I know whose it is, who owns the bank loan, but I have no illusions about who it belongs to in a wider sense – to a huge community of people whose engineering skill created it, whose mechanical skills maintain it, whose marketing skills convinced me it was cool to drive it. I can't get behind the wheel without remembering the people who taught me to drive and, even before that, the truck drivers in the Maori community I grew up in on the East Coast who would take me off during school holidays to help load the hay and the stock and, much less fun, the superphosphate bags. Through all of that I learnt to love the rhythm of the road, to time the revs and keep the gear changes clean and quick.

When you drive a truck, whoever you are, you automatically join an accepting community. Other drivers salute you with a flick of the hand on the wheel. You're expected to be someone who has their feet on the ground and knows a thing or two about how the world works. Which is very different from how you're treated when you appear conspicuously religious. Then it's as though you're seen to be suffering from some chronic illness that blurs your vision and dulls your appetite for what's going on in the world.

It's a lot more fun to drive a truck than to play a spiritual role. And a lot more human. And that's a pity. Because Kiwi spirituality is all about being fully human, living life with abundance and passion. All that people interested in spirituality are claiming is that they have glimpsed a vision of the way the world could be, the way that God made it and intended it. And if a truck reminds me of that, why then should a truck not be seen as a graceful thing?

If every time I drive my truck I am reminded of a community of people, Maori and Pakeha, whose skill and patience made me and fashioned me, who stay with me when the weather's bad and the journey's hard, and even if I drive through the valley of danger, their stories comfort me, why then should a truck not be seen as a graceful thing?

CHAPTER 11

Redrawing the maps
– the Spirit of MMP

If we followed the maps of the Old World, then New Zealand sailed off the edge of the chart on election night 1996 when it voted in its first MMP (mixed member proportional) government. We're sailing in waters now that the old mapmakers filled by drawing sea monsters, for want of anything else to put in the space.

The money markets watch our progress as a nation nervously, our political leaders put up a brave face to the world outside, yet inside we all know that we may as well be drawing sea monsters ourselves, for all the clarity we have about what lies ahead.

It wasn't just that we changed the voting system. The shift to MMP served only to bring to the surface a whole lot of changes that had been bubbling away for years. The election simply threw them up, like Ruapehu during one of its eruptions. The years that followed have made us forget our weariness with the old tankbuster style of politics by confrontation and the old two-party ideology that re-quired every issue to be left or right.

We take for granted now the flow-on from the Maori renaissance which has changed the cultural landscape of New Zealand, and which is now slowly being translated into a redistribution of dollars and cents, and rights over land and sea.

Also absorbed is the huge impact of the women's movement at every level of New Zealand life – from the way we meet and speak and make decisions in the workplace to the balance of our govern-ment. Finally, over a century since women won the vote, we have a critical mass of women in parliament, Pakeha, Maori, Asian New Zealanders, determined to make a difference together.

And along with all that there is the shift in power away from rural to urban New Zealand, from south to north, and the continued Aucklandisation of the country – trends that MMP may end up making worse if we're not careful.

All these forces bubbled up to the surface on election night back in 1996. We knew about them all before, but suddenly there they all were, popping up on the computer screens, and nobody, not even David Lange or Ruth Richardson, not even Ian Fraser, who is paid to have the right word for every occasion, could make much sense of where it was all taking us.

The eagerly awaited election coverage proved to be an anti-climax. We should have been prepared to enter the new land of uncertainty we had voted for, but the old hunger for clear outcomes, strong winners and sorry losers lingered on. The breakdowns in TVNZ technology, with candidates being asked to comment on conversations they couldn't hear, became a parable of the mismatch between old maps and new territory.

There has been much talk about the new breed of politicians we need for the world of MMP and the new skills of consultation they require, but there is no talk at all about the new breed of mapmakers we need to chart our way through these unknown waters, and the discipline they will require to interpret the new social, cultural and spiritual forces erupting across our landscape.

There are, of course, several groups with their hands up, offering their services as mapmakers for the MMP era. All the journalists for a start, who presumed to lead us through the first past the post days, are confident they can make the switch. But their performance to date suggests they are trying to sew old patches on to new wineskins. Their spirituality is still anchored in the old adversarial images of the bullfight and the boxing ring.

Another group who offered to lead us through the desert of uncertainty to the promised land beyond was the Christian Coalition. It's still not clear why they fared so badly at the polls and why it will therefore be hard for them to play this mapmaker role. Part of the reason is the suspicion our very secular society has of any religious voice that dares to speak up outside the sanctuary, especially if there is an edge of moralism or judgement or self-righteousness in that voice.

The lessons from the past are simple enough: if you want to preach, or if you want to manage change by confrontation, then you won't win friends and influence people in this new era. You probably won't be much use in drawing new maps and, even if you try, your directions are likely to lead people astray.

I don't know who these new mapmakers might be, but I do know we're going to have to widen our circle to find them, way beyond the ranks of the familiar and the photogenic commentators we presently rely on. We'll need to take more time to listen to wiser, older voices, and make more effort to hear directly from those who are hurting most, and watch more carefully what is happening to our landscape, rural and urban.

When I walk home at night from the cathedral where I work, in respectable, traditional, downtown Christchurch, I pass three restaurants, Indian, Mexican and Hare Krishna, two takeaways that provide the staple diet for hundreds of young people, two massage parlours, a live sex shop and an adult video parlour, a chapel for Japanese weddings, a TV company in a hurry to move to Auckland, a finance agency for people the banks won't lend to, the office of a highly politicised animal rights organisation drawing in many young members, and the headquarters of the Masonic Lodge, where new members are much harder to find, and up to a dozen young prostitutes huddled in doorways.

There's a glimpse of the new face of stuffy old Christchurch for you, all in two blocks. Is it any wonder that we found ourselves in uncharted territory with MMP? Somehow all these places I walk past are providing jobs and community and hope as well as alienation and despair for thousands of citizens of this proud garden city. Yet it's hard to hear the public voices of any of the people I walk past, let alone anyone who can explain how all these changes in our culture came about, so quickly.

Our religious traditions offer us no ready explanation or easy licence to become the new mapmakers. They warn us in stories like the one of the disciples meeting Jesus on the Emmaus Road and not recognising him, that familiarity with the old ways is no help for seeing the new reality and that even the best placed, best trained people miss the point of what's going on.

But I think that Emmaus Road story says something more. Perhaps it's also suggesting that in the most ordinary and everyday parts of our life, and through the new people we meet, even the ones we find unfamiliar and inconvenient and threatening, God might well be opening us up to wider ways of seeing what's happening in Aotearoa New Zealand.

The map of the world the Wizard used to sell in Christchurch's Cathedral Square showed New Zealand on top and Europe down below. It made its point at a time when we were still struggling to stop seeing ourselves as England's offshore island. For the MMP era, we need a map that is not only upside down, but also inside out. Who will draw it?

Certainly people who are confident and clear about their spirituality and accepting of the different ways that spirituality can be expressed, both inside and outside traditional religion. Such people could form a community of interest that urges time and patience for new maps to be made, that warns against cheap, quick and easy revisions of the old drawings, that laughs at ancient superstitions about lurking sea monsters, that refuses to buy maps of the whole country made in Auckland, and that welcomes new hands at the drawing board: Maori and Pakeha, women and men, new immigrants and old, angry and satisfied, Christians and people of other living faiths – and of no faith at all.

If we could change the way we think about unexplored territory and uncharted seas, who knows, this MMP era might prove to be the most creative time in our history, a time when we found new eyes for seeing, new hands for holding on to the Kiwi Spirit.

CHAPTER 12

Creation, listen to it groan
– rethinking the place of work

This book tries to express a spirituality that doesn't depend on church language. The Kiwi Spirit it names is not under Christian control. But there are words in the Judaeo-Christian tradition that we can all claim, regardless of our allegiance, or lack of it, to that tradition. Here are three, widely used in secular settings, that we can employ in our search for a homegrown spirituality: vocation, creation, sacrament.

The classic definition of sacrament was some material thing with an 'outward and physical sign with an inward and heavenly meaning'. We applied it rather narrowly to the sacraments ordained by the church – the water of baptism, the bread and wine of Eucharist – and thereby excluded those traditions that didn't value those rituals in the same way. But there is much more at stake if you take the Genesis story seriously and believe that the whole world God made is good, regardless of whether our engagement with that physical world results in blessing or curse.

Judith Rock, writing as a dancer and an artist, argues that 'the physical world may not be the only reality, but it is the theatre of revelation and is itself, as the physical source of form, a source of grace. As every child with a skinned knee knows, the physical world is a place of bane and blessing equally. Physical events in the ongoing drama in the theatre of revelation . . . extend into the mystery of God.'

The pen or the spade, the computer key or the tea towel, the steering wheel in our hands and the earth or concrete beneath our feet, all have the potential, if we choose to use it and see it, to be channels of God's grace.

The worker priest movement that took root in the factories around Paris in the 1930s was an awkward and short-lived experiment, finally closed down by the Vatican, but not before it created a legacy of inspiration about the holiness of material things. Scottish Presbyterian student Alastair Hulbert and several others from the Student Christian Movement revisited those same factories in the early 1960s. Alastair wrote about his experience of working as a welder, using the physical stuff of the trade as the basis for connecting not only with fellow workers, but also with the work itself. Listen to this good Calvinist using the language of sacrament:

> Gradually I began to get a feeling for metal, and discover the satisfaction of argon welding: this ball of molten steel which is the weld, that you control with your electrode and in which you regularly dip the filler metal, leaving behind tiny waves of steel – white, red, purple (all the colours of the liturgical year) – this ball which follows the arc as the sea obeys the moon, leaving behind the imprints of its ripples on the sand at low tide. There was born in me, all frail, a relationship with matter, where the co-ordination of eyes and hands, rather than reflection and speech, served as intermediary.

Such a sacramental view of the world has the power to break all sorts of captivities that limit our understanding of creation. The captivity that comes from the management culture, for example, controlled by the values of efficiency, rationality, success, and the appearance of control, forged in the boardrooms of Coca-Cola and Dow Chemical.

Spiritual values can prove to be subversive in such settings. Yet they need not be impractical or otherworldly. Agencies like the YWCA, the Women's Refuge movement, Greenpeace, the Friends of Tibet all manage to promote unpopular agendas about spiritual connections to mainstream society and provide some useful role models.

The threat of captivity doesn't come only from the management culture. The very work we do day by day can overwhelm us, especially in economies like ours where a few have too much work, and too many have not enough. Work is either hopelessly overvalued to the point of letting it kill us, or undervalued till it goes unrecognised and un-rewarded and we are demeaned and destroyed by its absence. Karl Barth wrote that in 'human work . . . there is built up an apparently independent world of human capacity, enterprise and achievement. This construction conceals heaven from us . . . and conceals God himself, so that people think they see in their [workplace] culture the

God who they must serve.' The old-fashioned word for that is idolatry.

The best counter to this risk of captivity from work itself comes from reclaiming another word from the Judaeo-Christian tradition that goes right back to the Genesis story of creation. In that account we are offered the job of becoming co-creators with God, through the roles of gardener, farmer, procreator, steward, guardian, traveller and settler, builder, artist. The list goes on as the biblical narrative unfolds and the work of the people of God keeps expanding in order to share in the unfolding of creation itself.

The New Testament passage that gives climactic expression to that process is the eighth chapter of Romans, in which we are all caught up in the groaning of creation as it struggles toward the fulfilment of new birth. But it is the First Testament that gives divine value to our work as co-creators. Rabbi Lionel Bleu, in a book entitled *To Heaven with Scribes and Pharisees*, says,

> The Jewish servants of God in this world are not perfect knights, or lonely hermits, but the holy company of righteous businessmen, the pious organisers of communities, the committee men, and apparatchiks who give their time and energy freely; the heroes who attend to the details of the world, and keep it going, for it does not go round by itself. As they do their holy work, the holiness rubs off on them, and makes them holy too. Provided they are working for God, and not for their own glory or ambition, this is their path to salvation. Over the concentration camp entrance the Nazis hung a sign, 'Arbeit macht Frei' (work makes free). This was terrible because it distorted a truth, which is one of the deepest in Jewish experience, about salvation, to which daily work, honestly done, is the door.

The material world, Bleu points out, is not only our workplace; it is the material we work with. 'No artist, no craftsperson, can despise his own tools, the medium he works in. No Jew can ever really deplore or despise the world. It can irritate him and hurt him, but he cannot reject it. Even wanting to do so would be irreligious.' Only when we have accepted our place, earned our living, can we 'turn to other realities, and worlds which certainly exist'. These are 'the joys of a religious retirement, which most of us have yet to earn.

In the meantime we get on with the job.'

Bleu finishes with a marvellous story of a learned eighteenth-century rabbi called Elijah, the Gaon of Vilna, who was giving a tutorial. Two of his pupils looked out of the window at a bird soaring in the sky. He asked one of them, 'What were you thinking, as you watched the bird?' 'I was thinking of the soul ascending to heaven,' the boy replied. Elijah thought, and asked him to leave the class. He smelt the mysticism of Jewish Poland. He turned to the other boy, and asked him the same question. The boy considered. 'If that bird dropped dead, and fell between two fences,' he said, 'who would own the body?' His teacher replied, 'God be praised, for someone who knows what religion is about!'

In our ordinary, everyday, down-to-earth wheeling and dealing and wondering how to make ends meet and keep the kids happy and hold out till Christmas, we are in fact sharing in the creation itself, for better or worse. We're either helping to further it or to destroy it. There is no neutral place for co-creators to stand. It's even dangerous to guess whose work is more important to creation. 'Who knows?' says Rabbi Bleu. 'Each of us is given their own work, and until we have done it, this is the highest for us.'

The work that engages us in daily contact with the physical world, whether or not we are lucky enough to get paid for it, has traditionally involved the idea of a calling or vocation. My favourite definition of 'vocation' is one used by Alastair Campbell in his book *Paid to Care*: the 'call from the creator God to fit in with the flourishing and fulfilment of all created things'.

It's a noble idea, and a liberating one when we apply it to every form of work, not only those honoured by the church. The Reformers of the sixteenth century are credited with releasing vocation from the exclusive control of religious orders and dignifying every kind of work as a holy calling. 'What you do in your own house,' said Martin Luther, 'is worth as much as if you did it up in heaven for our Lord God.' John Calvin reinforced that claim. 'In following your proper calling, no work will be so mean and sordid as not to have a splendour and value in the eye of God.'

This is all well and good but its potential for romanticism is endless. If your work is smelly, back-breaking, demeaning, then to describe it as vocation becomes very difficult. George McLeod once said he always took on the job of cleaning the latrines so 'I will not be tempted to preach irrelevant sermons on the dignity of all labour'.

The word vocation needs some careful attention before we throw it about in today's workplace. There are some forms of work that do not lead to the fullness of life and the flourishing of creation. The value of hard work does not cancel out the evils of exploitation and inhuman conditions. The so-called Protestant work ethic has too often been used as a camouflage for excesses of free-market economics, justifying greed and expediency with moralistic calls by the Business Roundtable to work harder and longer.

A closer look at the Reformers that we hold responsible for this ethic shows they were not so glib and naive as to see all work as God ordained. Work for them was never an end or a justification in itself; it was justification by faith not works that the Reformation was all about. Work for them was a duty, a simple necessity as part of the human condition, much as the New Testament sees it. It is God who bestows, and any success we enjoy is to be seen as blessing, not as self-made reward.

Any fulfilment and joy we get from work comes as a result of the service to others and to God that we're able to offer through our work. That's where the liberating Reformation insight lies – that through our work, no matter how ordinary or badly paid or not paid at all, we are able to connect with and contribute to the wider community, even the creation itself and its rhythms of toil and rest, rediscovery and recreation.

The concept of vocation has been much misused. Far from setting us up for disappointment and cynicism, vocation can be a word to free us from imprisonment by our immediate 'conditions' of the workplace so that we can see what we do as a connection with a wider community and a wider world, whatever the boss might say or the employment contract dictate. Wherever I am and whatever I do at work, I can still claim a calling to connect with those wider realities and enjoy the dignity and the strength that flows from that link. These traditional words – creation, sacrament, vocation – offer us a way out of the captivity that threatens us if we rely on the language of free-market economics or the management culture of efficiency at any price.

Each of these words leads into the hardest of current debates. Creation leads us right into the sustainability debate and the limits and redirection on work set by our environment and its non-renewable resources. Work that is out of sync, that defies the rhythm of the natural world, sows our destruction, as the Genesis story says so graphically.

Vocation is about connection with a wider community, making covenants and partnerships. Our calling is never to isolation or to self-serving. To work in Aotearoa New Zealand, under the umbrella of a treaty, using resources governed by that treaty, promises to become a lot more complicated in the next decade. We're going to need understandings of work that link us with each other, Maori and Pakeha, in alliances of justice and mutual respect.

As for sacrament, it can be the richest word of all, provided we can liberate it from an exclusively religious captivity. If we could begin to find a language to describe the physical world around us so that its sacramental potential could be seen and heard, then I believe the common spiritual vision we seek could come to birth more quickly and easily in Pakeha New Zealand. For that vision is not something that we have to invent; it comes from touching and seeing what is already there, something we can't see for looking.

Zoe White is an English Quaker who writes about the sacredness of all work and the power of all workers to be spirit bearers. She describes an old coal miner she knew who befriended the rats in the tunnels underground, by learning to listen to them, and to the wooden beams in the ceiling of the narrow shafts. 'When the beams start creaking,' he said, ' you know there is too much weight. And when the rats stop squeaking you know something's going to happen and you get out fast.'

That miner, for Zoe White, became a spirit bearer, a co-creator, a sacramental channel through which the great mystery of creation and transformation was taking place. If we could see our life in Aotearoa New Zealand through Zoe's eyes, even the most ordinary and domestic activity would radiate with spiritual purpose and power.

CHAPTER 13

Past the pub and the playing field
– the sense of silly rituals

In every church building I've worked in, no matter how modest and small, people turn up from nowhere to tell me, almost as though I should remember the occasion, that they attended a service here in 1931, or knew someone who was buried from here, way back when. For them, the building houses, before everything else, the memory of a ritual that has stayed with them and, in some strange way, has shaped their life ever since.

In our ever so secular Kiwi society, these religious rituals are made to seem a little silly. Television stereotypes them as the preserve of elderly, eccentric and inadequate people led by clergymen inclined to simper nicely and clergywomen inclined to giggle nervously. Yet, despite their seeming uselessness, these rituals are shamelessly copied, without credit, by every other part of society.

Take, for example, the world of sport, especially as it becomes more professional and commercial by the day. There are holy places and hallowed grounds, there are protocols for where best to sit and what to chant and wear and eat while you watch. There are the recitals of the saints who went before in the game, and dreams and visions of how it might be, if only, if only… There are images and icons of players whose endorsements earn thousands and make millions, souvenir photos and T-shirts which draw veneration and religious respect with an intensity that would embarrass most religious worshippers.

We play a shadow game with rituals in our society. We pretend we don't need them, then clutch on to them like drowning people grabbing at anything that floats. We see people who say they aren't interested in faith indulging unknowingly in the silliest of ceremonies and spending money on 0900 phone line astrological services and on mail order formulas for instant success and happiness.

With ritual, we are betwixt and between, caught between ignoring it altogether and taking it too seriously, losing the element of fun that good ritual has, the sense that it is only a game that we don't have to play, the freedom that it gives us to do something unnecessary. Physically, we can live without ritual. Spiritually, we hunger for it. For the nourishment that ritual gives is food for the soul.

Jesus didn't have our problem. He was like us in every way, beginning as a baby, as he is in the gospel story about the presentation of Jesus. Just over a month old, he would have been, when his parents brought him to the temple in Jerusalem. Eight days after his circumcision and after the forty days that his mother Mary had to stay at home after the birth of a male child (twice as long for a female child). For her purification and for the baby's naming and dedication she came with her husband to present a sin offering to the temple; preferably a lamb but, as they couldn't afford that, a couple of turtledoves or young pigeons would be acceptable to the priest.

Every detail of this ritual, every permitted variation, was laid down in the law of Moses that was followed by every Jew. The really pious ones, like the Pharisees and Sadducees, obeyed every jot and tittle of the law. But every Jew respected the basic rituals that Mary and her baby went through in this story.

This is God's truth grounded in the rituals of a first-century culture. That's where it starts, but not in order for us to imitate the details. Circumcision and purification ceremonies are no longer required. Even strictly orthodox Jews have trouble following every first-century detail. What we are being asked to do is trust that God is as present in our rituals of naming and renewing and belonging and blessing and empowering, as present in the ordinary detail of our timetables and words and actions as God was for those first-century people.

For Pakeha people that seems to be very hard. It's made harder by the fact that most of our rituals are borrowed from somewhere else. The current interest in retracing ancestral roots and drawing family trees is an attempt to reclaim a spiritual past that will make our rituals feel less borrowed and second-hand. Trouble is, most of us have to leapfrog backwards over several generations to make the connection with our Yorkshire grandma or our Norwegian great-granddad. And even if we succeed, the problem still remains of finding rituals that work in this time and place. So we continue to struggle with Christmases designed for cold winter days and Easter celebrations of spring replayed in autumn.

Gradually, the rituals will change as we modify old ones and invent new ones. So we're learning how to offer services that bless relationships as well as marry people for as long as they both shall live. With the help of our Maori partners, we're learning how to bless the houses we live in and to reconsecrate them in times of crisis. Something has shifted in the Kiwi psyche when you see sceptical middle-class couples invoking prayers like this one over their suburban bungalows: 'Encircle this dwelling place with your protection, O God; may your holy angels encompass these walls'. We're very gradually learning how to mark the rites of passage when we find jobs, and especially when we lose them, when we enter relationships and when we leave them, when we leave school and leave home, when we take up responsibilities and when we let them go.

Our various religious traditions contain a huge but often buried heritage of rituals to mark the external changes in our community – the seasons and harvests, endings, beginnings and anniversaries. We need to build an equally rich heritage of liturgies that mark the internal changes in our lives, our personal and collective rites of passage as we discover what it means to belong here in this land as Pakeha and Maori, women and men; what it is we need to let go and leave behind, what we can justly celebrate, what dreams of the future excite and unite us.

A Kiwi spirituality needs to be anchored and embedded in rituals that work and belong here. Otherwise we end up with a privatised and isolated faith that doesn't connect us with the people and the world around us. But the best established Kiwi rituals would be embarrassed to identify with anything spiritual or religious. The rituals of Kiwi life in the pub or on the playing field, over a cup of tea at the kitchen table, on a bush tramp or a fishing trip, at a hospital bed or a committee meeting, each have a built-in and well-defined set of boundaries and opportunities. The kinds of questions you can ask, the degree of physical closeness, the kind of humour allowed, the latitude given to newcomers, the clothing that's appropriate, how you bring a plate or buy a drink.

It's the intimate detail of those rituals that holds the clues to what really is distinctive about the Kiwi Spirit, clues that our writers and artists, filmmakers and musicians prise open for us. If we wanted to speed up the search for a confident and exclusive national identity, then the way to do it would be to commission fifty more New Zealand films and a hundred plays, twenty symphonies, ten dance performances, a dozen photographic exhibitions, twenty novels, ten new anthologies of poetry (five from the North Island, five from the South), all with no other brief than to reflect what's going on around us. And then we'd see more clearly where the Kiwi Spirit is moving, and the way to assemble and anchor the rituals to let us celebrate that Spirit would be so much easier to find.

Chapter 14

Spilling out all over
– Kiwis as passionate people

Poet Allen Curnow writes of a little boy, back in the days when barnstorming pilots charging for a joy ride were as much part of a country show as the horses and prize sponge cakes, who is desperate for a flight. 'Please, yes, let me,' begs the boy. 'My father hesitates, I pull and don't let go. Neither does the soul of the world, whatever that is … I'm lifted up and over and into an open cockpit. Contact . . . the chocks kicked clear, my balaclava knits old sweat and foul oil, where tomorrow encloses me now.'

That hunger to break free and do something expansive and liberating is a major theme of Kiwi spirituality, often violently expressed as it struggles to breathe in the suffocating air of religious respectability and conventional morality. Mid-century New Zealand writers constantly railed against these constraints that were often lumped together under the heading of Puritanism – a blanket term that was as much to do with materialism, smugness and hypocrisy as it was with a world-denying brand of religion. Frank Sargeson's short stories are the best-known battleground against these forces of Puritanism in Pakeha culture. He lines up parsons, politicians and civil servants, houseproud married women, wowsers and all good, respectable people as defenders of a stifling, spirit-killing lifestyle that was all pervasive in middle New Zealand. Those who manage to avoid or defy this deadly malaise are not the smart and successful but the crazy and the destitute, the misfits and the wanderers, and the children who are still able to respond instinctively to the wonder of the world.

Even if Sargeson is only half right, it's a bleak legacy that we inherit. One effect of such a background is to lower our expectation that the Kiwi Spirit can produce much by way of passion and exuberance. And when that passion does come, it will be unexpectedly and very briefly enjoyed by the least likely people. Like R.A.K. Mason's old swagger, the 'cold wet dead-beat' brought inside so we can 'put silk on his body' and 'slippers on his feet', feed him and offer him spiced wine. This royal treatment is warranted because, for Mason, the 'old lag' with his 'clumsy swag made of a dirty old turnip bag' is Christ himself.

Other more recent New Zealand writers don't have to push so hard or make such huge leaps to let the passion break through. Journalist and novelist Lindsey Dawson, describing her life, says that most of the time it is restrained and controlled, but there is another side. 'I have had times when I have had spiritual bursts, I suppose you would call them. It's not religion. It's more of a time for reflection and a time when I am full of wonder at what life is all about.' She describes one such burst in connection with the loss of a very close friend in a plane crash: 'during the period of grieving I did a lot of praying, which was something I had never done before. I had a dream one night, of the world as this great glistening, blue globe hanging in the dark in space, surrounded by this glittering web, like a measure of energy.'

As an authentic Kiwi spirituality evolves, perhaps it will become easier to tap into these pools of inspiration and delight. One reason that so many New Zealanders find anything to do with religion and spirituality so unattractive is that it appears so barren and joyless. The biblical images of heavenly banquets and choirs of angels are so far from any hint of present-day reality that they communicate only as Monty Pythonesque farce.

Yet a spirituality without passion and the ability to link us with the extravagant and the sublime is bankrupt before it begins. Thomas Moore defined passion as our capacity to be affected as much by the gentlest as the roughest experiences. It is this ability and willingness to be affected that provides the essential energy of the soul.

New Zealanders are not short of this capacity for passion, despite all the old stereotypes of being a constrained and subdued people. In the early 1970s Gordon McLauchlan wrote a study of our national character entitled *The Passionless People*. It doesn't make convincing reading today. The hunger for dramatic religious experience evidenced in the growth of the Pentecostal churches, the popularity of intense small group experiences for therapy, education and recreation, the success of extravagant festivals to celebrate wine, exotic food and music, the taste for the extreme edge of sporting life, and the fondness of TV commercial makers for the party image to sell everything from Lotto tickets to house paint – all these are indicators that passionate expression is part of the Kiwi experience.

As never before, a penchant for risk taking and boundary pushing is evident in Kiwi spirituality. The love of adventure, once funnelled off into going to war or the overseas trips in between, is evident now in the huge diversity of recreational and lifestyle options. Television programmes love to celebrate the trendy, photogenic face of these pursuits, but there is something more substantial going on in all this bungy jumping and jet boat riding, snowboarding and mountain biking, exotic gardening and cooking, body piercing and hair shaving. New Zealanders are hungry for a spirituality that reaches further, includes more, and lets us live more exuberantly.

The danger is that this passion will be captured by the media images and kept as the preserve of the young, the beautiful and the well-to-do. In his play *Inadmissible Evidence*, John Osborne addressed this danger with an angry, aging father telling his elegant, confident daughter just why her cool self-sufficiency upsets him: 'Such charm, such ease, such frozen innocence,' he rants at her. 'When you leave you'll have no rattlings or share of death, there'll be no little sweating, eruptions of blood, no fevers or clots or flesh splitting anywhere or haemorrhage. You'll have done everything well and sensibly and stylishly. You'll know it wasn't worth any candle that ever burned. You will have to be blown out, snuffed, decently, and not be watched spluttering and spilling and hardening.'

At present there is little evidence of older and younger New Zealanders recognising that they have a shared stake in the newly visible passion of the Kiwi Spirit. It's easier to see now because diversity of style and exuberant expression are more acceptable. But this didn't happen overnight. It grew out of the shared experience of thousands of New Zealanders whose lives of bold exploring, generous giving, self-disclosing, forward thinking, boundary testing have made it easier for us to be a passionate people today.

My admiration overflows for those who live in
big-screen Technicolor and Dolby sound,
open ocean racers and high-rise architects,
all-weather climbers and zany fashion designers
and the people who win the whatever award of the year.
They risk and reach for more
than my tidy life contains.
I trim new edges while
they plant new lawn.
I'd like to do something memorable for God.
The faith I hold does say it can be so,
to meet believers who have dreams to burn and
songs to sing that march us off to rainbow wars
and, when we sink, will float us off again.

Chapter 15

The grace of place
– finding where we belong

Some places in Aotearoa New Zealand have to be measured by more than the value of their real estate. Places defined by memories are obvious examples; where a love affair began or a child grew up can never be the same again.

But the power of some places goes beyond the residue of conscious memories. Pig hunting in an unfamiliar area of the Urewera Ranges behind Gisborne, I once came across a hillside clearing in the bush that had an overwhelming quality of presence and foreboding. Something had happened there quite outside my life and experience. To linger in that clearing was to get involved with something beyond my competence and control.

Little wonder that buildings where terrible things have happened, such as a mass killing, are routinely burnt and cleared so that a new start, in spiritual as well as physical terms, can be made on the site. But, more often than not, we don't have the luxury of burning down or walking away to begin again somewhere else. Places have to be reclaimed, renewed and rearranged so life can go on.

Place has always been a spiritual category for Pakeha people. It's just that we haven't found the vocabulary or given ourselves the permission to express it, for fear of sounding primitive or pagan. The eloquence of Maori voices in singing the spiritual power of their places has also been a little intimidating for Pakeha, and where the rightful ownership land itself under the Treaty of Waitangi is still in dispute, any spiritual assertions inevitably have a political edge. It quickly becomes a contradiction to sing a home-grown hymn such as Colin Gibson's 'In this familiar place, I know the mystery of your grace', when the place in question was confiscated in a land war a century before and its legal ownership is being argued in courts and tribunals.

The concept of turangawaewae – a place to stand with dignity – is needed as much by Pakeha as it is by the tangata whenua, the people of the land. Sadly, the Treaty of Waitangi, our best hope for that double dignity, is still resisted by many as an obsolete and unnecessary document. Legally, it is hard to interpret for today. Spiritually, its relevance is immediate and urgent.

H. A. Williams put it like this: 'The place where we feel most at home, the people we most deeply love, the works of genius that have fired our imagination, these are the instances of the Word make flesh and dwelling among us, and thus creating us'. People we love, and works of genius, readily become vehicles of Kiwi spirituality. Physical places, for Pakeha people, make us pause. Most of us have moved around the country. Our families are scattered and, after a generation or two, our heritages must reach back over oceans. Few of us enjoy taproots that go down deep in one place. Our root systems have had to spread wide and thin and shallow. But lots of strong trees thrive and hold their own on such systems.

A Kiwi spirituality has to revalue the ground under its feet. It may prove to be holier than we imagined. In an experimental liturgy called the Canterbury Service, Christchurch Cathedral has been attempting just such a revaluing. The service opens with this prayer:

> God of every place
> You meet us now within this place
> Inside the shelter of these stones
> and the hull of wood above.
> The rock and timber of Canterbury
> was formed by your hand
> and crafted by our forebears
> to form this Cathedral Church.
> It was built by men and women
> who trusted your presence then
> as we do here and now.
> Meet us again this night
> through the light and shadows,
> the space and symmetry of this place.

After that opening invocation, the service goes on to celebrate the life and work of Canterbury people, all the while anchoring the music and readings in a clear sense of place. Visual images of the landscape are projected while the following prayer is read aloud:

> Creator God
> You lay out a quilt of cultivation across our plains
> You braid our rivers
> You wait in the silence and snow of the high country
> And on the far horizon beyond our beaches
> Be with all the people of our region;
> In the empty places
> And the cities and the towns.
> Be with us as we work and wait for work,
> As we build and trade and farm
> And teach and nurse and cook
> And sing and play.

Those who attend the service are left, at the end, with a vivid sense of belonging that can be uncomfortable, even disturbing for some. Is it proper to be quite so forthright about the holiness of the ground beneath our feet? Most religious traditions have kicked for touch in answer to that question, preferring a more universal God, more likely to be found everywhere than here, watching us from a distance.

The Canterbury Service connects by naming very specifically the ground beneath our feet. But we can make equally powerful connections with our time and place by creating silent spaces and relying on symbols, light and darkness to let people make their own links. At Christchurch Cathedral we've tried to do just that with a new service that uses hardly any spoken words. The event is called No Ordinary Sunday – a service of worship for people who don't go to church – and it has drawn an extraordinary response, largely from people who have little contact with organised religion. The service gives people space to let go, to remember and to face up to their future. Silence, choral and instrumental music, candles, fire and greenery are all employed in a very open-ended way, without any verbal description or prescription. Yet the effect is a powerful sense of anchoring in time and place.

Kiwi spirituality will flourish when we are bold enough to name aloud the places that we know already are hallowed ground. Surprisingly, some of the strongest guardians of such places are people who have least to do with organised religion. Such defenders of old churches, burial places and historic sites are often branded as superstitious traditionalists, but for them such venues are the only links with a spirituality that has disconnected with the rest of society. They may know more than the rest of us.

The power of some places defies our words. They require us to walk and talk more softly as we enter. Light enters more gently, outside sounds are subdued. Here we can find free space for the Spirit that recreates us and gives us new strength for standing straight in an upside-down world.

Chapter 16

Coping with community
– the intimacy muddle

It's a horse and carriage combination: the exhilaration and expectation that go with intense spiritual experience and the desire to share that experience and have it supported by others in community.

The risks of that community taking bizarre forms is well attested to by recent publicity about cultic suicide, sexual molestation and armed resistance within religious sects from California to Canterbury. We don't need too look far to find examples of spiritually minded people with the best of intentions creating communities with the worst excesses of manipulation and fear. A run of recent films – *The Crucible, Breaking Waves, The People versus Larry Flynt* – reveal a box-office fascination with this ability of religion to generate weird group dynamics and fanatical behaviour. In milder forms, many churches in New Zealand trade heavily on the language of family and the promise of close relationships, then wonder why people, especially in younger age groups, stay away in droves.

Any offer of community is accompanied in our Kiwi culture by a strong suspicion of intimacy and a fear of being forced into uncomfortable closeness. The negativity in Pakeha history towards all forms of organised religion is bound up with its lack of respect for space and choice and mobility. Religious groups invariably demand levels of commitment at a high level of personal intensity and intimacy, and for lengths of time that don't marry easily with the flux and flow of the rest of our lives. We enjoy and exercise a huge range of choice in the rest of our recreational time (which is where spirituality fits in). Our selection of social, sporting and cultural pursuits shows great diversity and mobility across all sorts of locations, tastes and styles. Our spiritual lives require at least the same room to move and demand permission to draw on several traditions at the same time.

In any community in Aotearoa New Zealand with some spiritual curiosity, you'll find a mix of incense and images from a Hindu tradition, meditation techniques and martial arts from a Buddhist tradition, rituals of welcome and gathering from a classical Maori tradition, ethics and music from a European Christian tradition, and a list of hybrid variations on all these sources and a dozen more, not forgetting an old-fashioned pagan festival or three. That's the context of our search for a Kiwi spirituality. It's not a journey for purists who want their inspiration untainted.

A healthy Kiwi spirituality, once it finds enough confidence to live with its mixed parentage, will need to encourage a whole variety of communal forms through which it can be expressed. Some of them will be intensive, highly disciplined and committed small groups. But the great majority of these shared expressions will be very loosely defined, highly mobile, constantly changing networks for sharing meaning, identity and mutual support.

Motorists on the West Coast are still linked by a common signal, one that all rural New Zealand drivers used thirty years ago – a simple lift of the finger on the wheel. The gesture doesn't pretend to promise any great commitment or common interest, though it does reassure you that if something went wrong on the road, there would be a fair chance of someone stopping to help. What the signal does is simply acknowledge the other motorist as someone sharing a journey, even though it is in an opposite and unknown direction. We need something like that lifted finger as a rite for seekers of Kiwi spirituality.

You could only just call it a community ritual, but we need such minimal commitments for a while to recover from the anxious and overheated intensity that so many religious groups labour under in our Pakeha culture. Minimal communities are part of our lives in so many areas, based on as little as the common experience of enjoying the same movie in different parts of the country. That two-hour experience enables a collection of total strangers to share a point of reference that enables communication to happen, T-shirt slogans to be shared and understood, and eventually wider dreams to be shared.

A community that could build a Kiwi spirituality needs only to offer a shared vocabulary, a sense of common direction and a respect for the variety of travellers making the journey.

What any spirituality offers at a deeper level than activities to perform or codes to obey is a way of seeing the world that is wider and deeper and richer than the conventional view. To use Benedict Groeschel's definition of spirituality, it is no more than letting 'all that takes place become part of the mystery of God's life with us'.

To do justice to such breadth, we need a vastly wider range of channels through which our spirituality can be expressed and named and recognised. Minimal forms of community, subtle badges and symbols of belonging to a common search or sharing a common sympathy are enough to be going on with. For we live in an in-between time. The shape of a new spirituality may well be emerging, but we have to live among the rubble of the old for the time being. This is not the time to claim too much or stand too close.

CHAPTER 17

Whose story is it anyway?
– telling it like it is

A young New Zealander who has never given the time of day to debates about Kiwi identity and felt more sympathy with a Coke bottle than with any national symbol, stands alone on a crowded street in Bangkok, short of money and friends, and starts to feel overwhelmingly connected with the homeland and friends she has gone overseas to escape. What was boring back there takes on a value and depth she has never imagined.

Bob Lowe of Fendalton and Taumarunui, on his first visit to London, proud of his agnosticism, attends a Christmas Eve service in a church, and out of the darkness a lone choir boy sings the opening lines of *Hark the Herald Angels Sing*. A tradition of faith that Bob had never seen as more than background noise suddenly lays claim on him and his life is changed forever.

Two friends who have lived in the same small town for years and shared all kinds of grief and joy together fall out with each other and say things that dismember their friendship and can't be taken back. Years later, they meet by chance in the street, have a cup of coffee together, and find enough shared memory to pick up their relationship again.

A well-known Pakeha artist is told his Hamilton exhibition is cancelled because it would be showing alongside a display of Tainui treasures. And whereas the Tainui display tells the story of a people, the Pakeha art is only that of an individual. So he is replaced with an exhibition of Goya, because that artist's paintings tell the story of the Spanish people.

A not so well-known English artist displays a statue of the Virgin Mary with a condom over her head in the opening exhibits of Te Papa. Several Christian as well as Muslim and Buddhist groups object violently, including the Anglican Bishop of Aotearoa, Whakahuihui Vercoe, who says you can't fool around with sacred objects.

The common thread in all these experiences is the word 'story'. Stories that people didn't know they had, let alone could redeem. Stories tightly held that can't be passed around, much less altered, without permission.

It's a good time to talk about such stories in a society hell bent on encouraging people to stand alone on their own two feet, free from any sort of state support or subsidy. The hero is the person who makes it as an individual; the Lone Ranger who comes home with a superannuation package and pictures of kids who have all graduated, found good jobs for life and paid off their student loans.

The sort of story that's fashionable at present is about individuals rather than groups, about what is happening now rather than what is evolving out of a history, and if there are stories to be shared, this is best done between people like us who enjoy the things that we do. Can you imagine mixing the people who frequent elegant eateries with the people you meet at the pub across the road? Or those who worship at the New Life Centre with the folks who love choral evensong?

The fashion of our time is to tell my story, or your story, but hardly ever our story, unless it's tailored for a niche market. And tailor we do, with a vengeance, especially in cities like Christchurch and Auckland. Church by church. Suburb by suburb. School by school. Job by job. Tribe by tribe, of both the Maori and the Pakeha kind.

That's all well and good but what we desperately need, alongside the safe and familiar stories we can own and control, are the epic ones that all sorts of unlikely people can claim. Big, broad stories that touch the roots of our humanity and our place in the universal and eternal frame of things.

Such stories can't be contained and packaged like an order from KFC. They're often unsettling, hard to control precisely because they connect with so many different people. The great struggle of our time is over the ownership of these wider stories.

We've got privacy laws to guard the personal stories, even a privacy commissioner with his own slot on National Radio. We've got copyright laws and the Fair Trading Act to protect the commercial stories. But the big stories that tap into the sources of our humanity and our spirituality, our womanhood and manhood; the stories that define our culture and the places we call home and give us the right to stand tall and strong and proud – all those are up for grabs.

In this postmodern, postChristian, postNew Zealand Post Office society, there is nowhere to go and no one to define orthodoxy for you. So the great stories of our heritage, the myths and the music and the art forms that have shaped our different cultures, float free in cyberspace, open to the highest bidder – fodder for the next TV commercial or advertising campaign.

Not everyone, of course, is quite as free with their stories. Tikanga Maori are much better organised and much more aware of the boundaries of ownership and the limits of exploitation. Pacific Island New Zealanders are testing those same boundaries and extending them a little, if the TV comedy and stand-up comedians in Auckland are anything to go by.

But Pakeha people are still floundering over what to do with their stories. Some are still wondering whether they have any distinctive story at all. And Christians are portrayed by the media as being in disarray over their story. The 400 who marched on Te Papa to protest the virgin in the condom are represented as speaking for the whole church.

We can blame the media for that, but we also have to blame ourselves for our failure to present any common witness to the community. We have tried to agree on too much. Now there doesn't seem to be any religious consensus on anything.

Our spiritual stories are in as much disarray as all our other stories. We need to get that sorted soon. Because if we don't own and honour our stories of spirituality, which tell us who we are and remind us of our heritage of faith and culture, then someone else will do the job for us. The Coca-Cola story will teach the world to sing if we don't teach ourselves. The government will provide a code of social responsibility for us if we don't get involved. Corporate sponsors will welcome us to our world, show us how to be one together and define the Kiwi Spirit on the hulls of multi-million-dollar yachts and rugby jerseys. If we don't join the shaping and the telling of our stories then the American tele-evangelists on TV channels mysteriously called Freedom will tells us what true religion is all about.

As never before, we need to be clear about our stories – Pakeha, Maori, New Zealander, urban, rural, north or south, women and men. If we're not clear, then we can't begin to talk to each other, for there is no neutral place in which to stand. We come to each other inside our stories. The love that will not let us go is always found within a story – a relationship, an event and a memory. The Kiwi Spirit always comes in that same story-bound way. And when we do get inside our stories, then love does take hold and the Spirit does move.

We've got lots of models for finding our stories. For example, there is the Jewish one that says whenever you've received something to be grateful for, like a good harvest, or a good run of work or a family celebration or, for that matter, when things go wrong and life is tough, then take the time to recite your history in a poem or a song. The Kiwi style might not so well organised or poetic but it's just as eloquent. In the awkwardness, the pain and ambiguity of our short Pakeha history, there is still plenty to be proud of, if only we will own it and try to understand it.

Nobody can deny us the right to tell our own stories that map the way the Kiwi Spirit moves in our midst. And the clearer we are about that, the easier it is to see where we fit in the universal human story.

CHAPTER 18

Not knowing is okay
– the blessing of uncertainty

Fashionable though it is – one day soon *Metro* magazine will do a cover story on it – spirituality is still a woozy topic in the minds of most New Zealanders. Not the sort of thing you'd launch into at the bar on Friday night or when the guests arrive for dinner.

'How's your spirituality been this week?' 'Oh, fine thanks. It slumped after the weekend but it's picked up.'

The unease is due not only to the endemic Kiwi suspicion of anything religious. It's also because of the elusiveness of the subject itself, about as slippery an eel as you can find. Now you have it, now it's gone. Because it's not right doctrine or right ethics or right ritual that defines spirituality. It's all about the practice of the presence of the holy. Understanding it, yes, but, more important, seeing, feeling and incorporating that presence in our bodies and our souls.

To know and grow that presence of the holy in our midst, sooner or later we each need to find the language and symbols of an established faith tradition, and the support of a community that shares a common vision. Kiwi spirituality alone is going to be pretty thin food for the journey, without the nourishment of a heritage of wisdom and the inspiration of a Jesus or a Buddha or a Mohammed.

But the beauty of having a Kiwi spirituality as a common ground, whatever our wider faith and however strongly we hold on to it, is that it provides a check on us taking religion too seriously and becoming so heavenly minded about our own brand of faith that we're no earthly use and make no common sense to the people we live and work with who don't share our convictions. (And, in a country where only 13 percent of the population have any strong religious attachment, that's an awful lot of people.)

A spirituality based simply on the time and place we all share and are equally entitled to; a spirituality that asks nothing more of us than the recognition that our immediate surroundings may be a window on a wider and deeper reality; that there is something distinctive about the way it appears here in Aotearoa New Zealand and nowhere else; and that such a spirituality, young and still evolving though it is, understated, modest and unencumbered, is all we need to be going on with – isn't that worth having? If you're locked into a religious tradition that has claimed all the answers and can't even hear the questions that outsiders are asking, or if you can't find a doorway into faith that doesn't threaten to jam your fingers, then this sort of Kiwi spirituality has to be good news indeed.

Its very refusal to be too confident or too precise has to be the best news of all. Because the greatest failing of all the established religious traditions is their inability to own their incompleteness and uncertainty. The built-in bias to a literal brand of fundamentalism is the common curse, however sincere and well intentioned the promoters usually are. What they can't see for looking is the way in which our experience of faith has been shaped by a scientific world view that demands empirical proof in order to believe anything and a consumerism which promises that I can buy satisfaction on my terms. I can have it all and I can have it now.

Such distortions are disowned by all religious traditions, but they survive and flourish because they are built into our Western culture. The beauty of a Kiwi spirituality, new coined by comparison, is that it challenges, from the outside, the arrogance of certainty that comes from the inside of religious creeds. New Zealand's religious history is littered with examples of competing denominations dividing families and communities, moralistic preachers coercing and threatening, theology being used as an obstacle to racial and gender equity, healthy sexuality, family planning, even the theory of evolution. The pretence of certainty has done enormous damage to religious understanding. A Kiwi spirituality that makes no such claims can fill a space, that no other movement seems able to occupy, without bitter division.

Even those of us who do stand strongly inside one or other faith tradition need this challenge to certainty that recalls us to our own historic roots. In his book *Passion for Pilgrimage*, Alan Jones summarises the wisdom that our respective heritages seem to have lost in the late twentieth century. St Augustine's words from the fifth century, for example: 'If you have understood, then what you have understood is not God'. And St Teresa of Avila's advice to one of her nuns who claimed to have seen the Virgin Mary: 'Never mind dear, it will go away'. This warning against certainty that denies the essence of faith as things hoped for is not confined to Christianity. The Buddhist dictum says: 'If you meet the Buddha on the road, kill him'.

A Kiwi spirituality that can discover and celebrate hints and glimpses of God's beauty and mystery in the landscape, history and community of this time and place, and that treats such insights as markers for the journey rather than shrines to stop and worship at; a spirituality that is worn lightly and easily and dares to be tentative and to unfold as we go – we urgently need that to understand the movement of the Spirit in Aotearoa New Zealand.

Reading list

*Publications referred to in this book and
commended for further reading*

Andrew, Maurice. *Responding in Community*, Faculty of Theology, University of Otago, 1990.

Baxter, James K. *Jerusalem Daybook*, Price Milburn, Wellington, 1971.

Belich, James. *Making Peoples*, Penguin Books, Auckland, 1996.

Bingen, Hildegaard, in *The HarperCollins Book of Prayers*, compiled Robert Van de Weyer, Castle Books, 1997.

Bleu, Rabbi Lionel. *To Heaven with Scribes and Pharisees*, Darton, Longman & Todd, London, 1975.

Brasch, Charles. 'The Silent Land', in *The Penguin Book of New Zealand Verse*, Penguin Books, Harmondsworth, 1960.

Chesterton, G.K. *Lunacy and Letters*, ed. Dorothy Collins, Sheed & Ward, London, 1958.

Culbertson, Philip (ed.). *Counselling Issues and South Pacific Communications*, Accent Publications, Auckland, 1997.

Curnow, Allen. 'Attitudes for a New Zealand Poet', in *The Penguin Book of New Zealand Verse*, Penguin Books, Harmondsworth, 1960.

Darragh, Neil. 'A Pakeha Christian Spirituality' in H. Regan and A.J. Torrance (eds), *Christ and Culture: The Confrontation Between Gospel and Culture*, T. & T. Clark, Edinburgh, 1993.

Dawson, Lindsey. *Angel Baby*, Hodder & Stoughton, London, 1995.

Delattre, Roland. *Beauty and Sensibility in the Thought of Jonathan Edwards*, Yale University Press, Yale, 1968.

Gibson, Colin. *Alleluia Aotearoa*, New Zealand Hymn Book Trust, Wellington.

Groeschel, Benedict J. *Spiritual Passages*, Crossroads, 1984.

Hulbert, Alastair. *One World*, Magazine of the World Council of Churches, Geneva, 1978.

Jones, Alan. *Passion for Pilgrimage*, Harper & Row, San Francisco, 1989.

Lineham, P.J. 'Protestant Piety in New Zealand', *Journal of Religious History*, Vol. 13, No. 4, 1985, pp. 370 ff.

Mason, R.A.K. *Collected Poems*, Pegasus Press, Christchurch, 1963.

McLeod, George F. *Only One Way Left*, Iona Community, Glasgow.

Mikaere, Buddy. *Te Maiharoa and the Promised Land*, Heinemann, Auckland, 1988.

Moore, Thomas. *Care of the Soul: A Guide for Cultivating Depth and Sacredness in Everyday Life*, HarperCollins, New York, 1992.

Osborne, John. *Inadmissible Evidence*, Faber & Faber, London, 1965.

Puls, Joan. *Every Bush is Burning*, World Council of Churches, Geneva, 1983.

Ramshaw, Gail. *Searching for Language*, Pastoral Press, Washington DC, 1988.

Webster, Alan. 'New Zealand Study of Values', paper presented at 1st Forum of the Conference of Churches of Aotearoa New Zealand, May 1988.

Wilbur, Richard. *The Poems of Richard Wilbur*, Harcourt Brace, New York, 1965.

Williams, H.A. *True Resurrection*, Mitchell Beazley, London, 1972.